TANYA TUCKER ON TANYA TUCKER:

"I am glad I came from nothing because it makes a better story."

"I'm sure everybody in town thought Billy Sherrill was nuts for signing a thirteen-year-old girl."

"I want to be labeled like an Elvis. I would love to be bunched with the best. After all, who is any higher than Elvis?"

"My bad reputation has done wonderful things for me."

"Being anywhere near a wedding gown makes me nervous."

"People know that I'm no flash in the pan, that I am going to be here for the long haul."

"I want to tour and record as long as I can breathe."

Tanya

ACE COLLINS

ST. MARTIN'S PAPERBACKS

TANYA

Copyright © 1995 by Ace Collins.

Cover photograph courtesy of the Country Music Foundation.

ISBN: 0-312-95614-2

Printed in the United States of America

St. Martin's Paperbacks edition/September 1995

10 9 8 7 6 5 4 3 2 1

To Jenny and Jeannie and all the others who work behind the scenes to make those in the spotlight shine!

- *Chapter One* -

Putting a Life Into Perspective

I am glad I came from nothing because it makes a better story.

—*Tanya Tucker*

Over the course of her thirty-six years Tanya Tucker has been a lot of different things to a lot of different people. She has been labeled everything from "child phenom" to "superstar" to "washed-up, drugged-out has-been" to "the comeback kid." She has been loved, despised, praised and cussed. And in the usually staid world of country music, she has been nothing if not controversial. Yet in the midst of life-style choices that stirred earthquakelike shocks throughout the Bible Belt and tabloid stories that have raised questions about every facet of her career and personal life, she has remained one of the industry's most honest and revered voices. In the face of overwhelming odds, she has not only held onto stardom, but has grown in stature.

With all this in mind, it goes without saying that Tanya Tucker is a complex personality. Yet, as you follow her you also find that in many ways she is simple and direct. The fact is that she often beats around the bush to get straight to the point. She is an outlaw who never runs, a friend who never wavers. She is a nineties woman who has quite publicly given birth to two children without benefit of a husband and yet is a very old-fashioned lady who speaks reverently of marriage and commitment. She has raised more hell than most leather-clad bikers, and yet she often speaks with friends and the press of seeking spiritual truth and searching for God's will for her life. She is Music City's rag sheet queen, but she is also the girl next door. She is a party animal and a doting mother. She has packed seventy years of hard living into half that amount of time, and yet, just like a schoolgirl on graduation night, she still innocently wonders if she will ever find her Prince Charming.

A trip down music row or the supermarket aisle or a Country Music Association convention can get you a solid feel as to who Dolly Parton, Barbara Mandrell and Reba McEntire are. A visitor from another planet could feel he knows these three woman by summations from these common sources. Their portraits are clear and the images consistent, but in Tanya's case it is a far different picture that is developed. Tightly focused one moment, abstract and defused the next, she is much too complex and her life has been far too disjointed to clearly put her in a slot. In her case no feelings, no views, no truths are unanimously held or accepted. There is too much ground to cover, too many different personas in the small, energetic frame. We can't and probably won't ever find a preformed niche in which to place her because she is always moving in so many different directions at the same time.

So who is Tanya Tucker?

If you were to get a dozen country music critics together in a room to talk about Tanya, a never-ending argument will begin as to what her contributions to the music business really were. Some would argue that she is one of the most important women to ever grace the stage of the Opry, others would view her as an overproduced former child star with limited musical talent who has ridden a gimmick to fame and fortune. And these diverse opinions would just be the first round of the arguments. Unlike most other major stars, she is both heavily admired and scorned, lifted up and exalted and at the same time written off. Few country music entertainers have created or probably ever will create such a wide disparity of opinions among the experts.

So who is Tanya Tucker?

If you pull her past and present friends together for an informal reunion there will also be a great deal of discussion and disagreement as to who this woman really is. Some will point out that she can be generous to a fault, while others will state emphatically that she is extremely selfish. A few will acknowledge a drinking problem which has never gotten under control, others will swear that she is a fitness nut who has left all her drug problems behind her long ago. Most will smile and talk about the long ago days of all-night partying, but a few will disagree, saying that image is not even close to the Tanya who loves to stay home with her children and read. The fact is that no two friends know her in the same way. She is somehow unique to each of them.

So who is Tanya Tucker?

Country music's musicians and artists are also divided on Tanya. Glen Campbell still sees her as the devil in black leather pants. Yet a host of others find her sweet, straightforward and bighearted. Some marvel at her commitment to her fans and her showmanship. But there are others who point out that she is very much a female Hank Williams—great or lousy, it just depends on the night you see her or if she shows up.

So who is Tanya Tucker?

More often than not writers have loved her when deadlines are near because she is so outspoken and honest. She gives them great quotes. Yet even those who have interviewed her a dozen times over twenty years are lost when they try to describe her. She is always changing, forever evolving, never predictable.

So who is Tanya Tucker?

Who knows?

The real Tanya Tucker may never be identified and

pinned down. She may never fit comfortably into a mold or wear a label. Yet fans, friends, industry insiders and the press can come together and agree on one thing. She is traveling her own road without benefit of a map. With this superstar there is no need for a map or a real master plan. She is a throwback to a time when performers operated on faith and instinct. Like a Texas tornado, she randomly chooses her spots, sits down quickly, and then leaves to let people question and wonder. In her stormy life she has touched down many times and impacted millions of people. Yet her path has been haphazard, her strikes both direct and indirect. And for those reasons and a few thousand more there is no country music forecaster who can predict where or with how much force she will next hit.

Yet in a career that has been rocky, a life that has been filled with unexplainable turns, in the midst of success and failure one thing has been self-evident and stable. One thing can be picked out without fear of argument or contradiction. One person who has always been there. He has been the rock, the glue and the wind. It goes without saying that without her father, Tanya Tucker would never have gotten to the spotlight, and without him coming back to her in times of deepest need, she probably would never have found her way back to that warm glow the second and third time.

Jesse "Beau" Tucker was the driving force behind the star, and Tanya's story is really as much about Beau's life, his love for his children, and his ability to put his own dreams on hold and reach for theirs, as it is about hit records and concert tours. If there is a constant in Tanya's life, then her father is it. And if there is a way to measure Beau Tucker, then it is by the accomplishments of his youngest daughter.

Jesse "Beau" Tucker was born in Colgate, Oklahoma, and at an early age moved to the small panhandle town of Denver City, Texas. He was a product of the times.

Much like the characters John Steinbeck made famous in *The Grapes of Wrath,* Beau and his family were desperately poor. These people were the product of the Dust Bowl. The winds that had swept away so much of their home state's soil also carried away their roots. The dreams they had were small because nothing was assured, not even knowing if a job would last more than a few days or if there would be food on the table the next week. No black-and-white *Life* magazine image, no matter how riveting, ever captured the insecurity and shattered spirit that had made old men and women out of folks who were robbed of their youth. But this was the rural America of that era and millions, including the Tuckers, were among the casualties.

The Tucker family, like hundreds of thousands of others, would roam the countryside picking cotton, doing odd jobs, finding any and everything they could just trying to make ends meet. To them the Great Depression was more than an expression, it was a way of life. No one had to tell them they were a long shot at ever knowing real security. They faced that fact each and every day. Christmas meant an apple or an orange. Birthdays meant a song and a slice of johnnycake. Times were tougher than modern folks can imagine, but maybe faith, love and family were tougher then than anyone could now imagine.

In the midst of great uncertainty punctuated by hard work and poor pay, the Tuckers were typical of the Okies who were uprooted and became nomadic pilgrims during this period. They had deep faith in themselves, a love for family, a belief that honesty and hard work were life's most important virtues, and a special inbred spiritual bond to their maker. They were tolerant of others, and open to new ways and ideas. They wanted to get ahead and would show this by outworking any of those around them, but they also knew that as long as they held their family together, they were, in a way, very rich and very blessed.

That special American richness of the heart was what must have sustained young Beau and a million others just like him, because even at a tender age he must have realized that his life and his dreams were to be put on hold for his family. Like so many others, Beau Tucker never had much of a boyhood, the depression and the situations it created didn't give him the time. He grew into a man quickly, one who could stand the test of time, hardship and pain.

Sixty years later, the idea of children working twelve-hour days in the fields with their dreams shattered before they could be developed, accepting the cruel blow of fate that robbed them of play and fun, would seem unthinkable. Yet without the complete acceptance of this unfairly dealt hand, Beau Tucker would not have made it through this time. And it would also be this strong commitment to the beliefs learned in the fields of his youth that would later allow him to step aside from his own life and goals and make his daughter's dreams come true.

Beau Tucker met a cute little Abilene-born girl named Juanita in Denver City, Texas. They had gone to grade school together until he had dropped out in fifth grade to work full time. Yet even though he was out of school, he kept up with one of this small and poor town's prettiest girls. Juanita, both shy and quiet, had little to do with the gruff, cocky Beau. She thought him a bit too arrogant, too sure of himself. She didn't like him much at all. Yet the times would eventually give her a chance to see him in a different light.

In spite of the best efforts of FDR and the New Deal, the depression in Texas didn't really end until the advent of World War II. With the war going on, jobs were easier to find and for the first time in a generation prosperity looked as if it were just around the corner. Beau was fourteen when he left town to work in a plant that had been energized by the battles on beaches and in fields so far away. As he sweated in the line, Beau was hoping that Juanita would pine for him while he was away, but she didn't much care. She barely even noticed that he wasn't coming around anymore. Yet a few months later, when he came home for a visit, Juanita took another look at the fifteen-year-old man-child. He seemed different, more mature, more responsible and much better looking. Now here was a man who could turn a girl's head. Juanita, though barely in her teens, thought she might have met her knight in shining armor.

For Beau, who had a steady job, a few dollars in his pocket and a goal to live better than he ever had, there was now a security in his life he had never really known. Yet he wanted more, he also had a dream of sharing his life with Juanita. So with the whole world in the midst of a war, the new fifteen-year-old Beau convinced the pretty brunette to marry him. Many in Denver City would frown and say that the couple was far too young. But the truth was that things were different then. The times had made kids grow up in a hurry, and with hundreds of thousands of people dying in the war that might last years, every teenager must have wondered how long anyone had left. "Doing it before it was too late," had become a new American motto. With that in the front of everyone's mind, things happened that wouldn't have happened a few years before. So, in a very small service, Beau and Juanita said, "I do," and no one close to them asked, "Are you sure?" They just wished them well and said a prayer for their happiness.

"He was a poor boy with a drive," Juanita would say as she later looked back on those simple days and that stark beginning. "He thought he could do anything." And no one in their right mind would try to tell him he couldn't. He was proud enough and strong enough to make them pay for their lack of faith.

After the war Beau had many jobs. For the young man the most consistently inconsistent opportunities presented themselves in the construction business. Already trained to operate heavy equipment, he moved from job to job, home to home, town to town and state to state tracking down work, staying until the job was completed and then moving on. With a new baby son Don and a young wife, it was a hard way to live. It would have probably torn a weaker marriage to pieces, but while this union bent, it never came close to breaking. Juanita loved Beau and she never looked back. People now marvel at this fact, especially today when marriages come and go as quickly as a summer breeze, but the hard times seemed to weld the Tuckers even closer together. The two really had become one for either the good or the bad, and even when the bad times far outweighed the good ones, they hung on.

"There were spots when it was real tough," Beau recalled, "but I got an education on a day by day basis. Still, what gives me all my willpower and drove me was my children." He wanted something far better for them than his folks had been able to give him. He wanted them to have a few dreams come true.

Beau was a big man with a temper. He was by this time in his life extremely strong. Those who didn't know him well thought of him as gruff, hot-blooded and stubborn. He was all of those things, but he was so much more. Demanding, he was also giving. His family knew that he expected them to toe the line, but they also knew that he loved them more than he loved life itself. He was fair, honest and loyal. He was also always looking for a way to do things in a better fashion, tap into an undiscovered vein of gold and mine it. He didn't know where his ticket out of poverty was, but he was always searching for it. He never gave up and settled for things the way they were. And those who knew him well realized that when he found that ticket, no matter how much of a long shot it was, he was not going to turn his back on doing whatever it took to make something big happen. That was the way Beau viewed the American Dream.

From the postwar years to the fifties, things continued to go financially up and down for the family. Beau's economic surges and false starts were due to his never finding anything other than what amounted to part-time employment. As an equipment operator he worked only on the construction of buildings, utility contracts and other specialized work which needed his services. To make ends meet during the off-season he would sell scrap metal, drill wells and do odd jobs.

Besides his family and his struggles, the one constant in Beau's life was his love for country music. He didn't sing much, other than imitating Ernest Tubb, but he did have a good ear for music. He seemed to have a natural gift that impressed both his family and friends for picking which new releases were going to be hits and which were going to be flops. His knack for recognizing sounds and material would come into play in a big way just a few years down the road, but for right now it was only family friends who'd say, "You outta be in Nashville producing hits." Of course it always brought a big laugh because who could ever picture big old Beau Tucker rubbing elbows with Marty Robbins and Ernest Tubb? That would never happen, all of them agreed.

By 1951 the couple's son Don was growing up fast, and in that year he was joined by a sister, LaCosta (while most agree on this year, some sources give LaCosta's birth date as late as 1956). With one more mouth to feed and the climb up life's mountain getting harder and harder, Beau should have seen that he was probably never going to get out of the rut in which most undereducated men usually found themselves. With the veterans going back to school on the GI Bill, with high-paying jobs now going to those who had the most education, this realization broke many men, but it is what drove Beau forward. He wanted something better for his family and he wasn't going to give up until he found it. Those around wondered why he didn't see the handwriting on the wall. What they didn't know was that he had seen it, but refused to acknowledge it. Beau simply believed that he could climb whatever mountain stood between him and giving his family something very special. Whatever it took, he would do it. No matter how bad the present looked, there was something better up ahead.

"We lived in matchboxes," LaCosta would later remember. "We lived in houses that were literally condemned." Yet, they got by without welfare, food stamps and handouts. It might be a very worn and overused description, but the Tuckers really were "poor, but proud."

By the time Juanita had become pregnant with their third child, the family was back in Texas and things had changed little. Beau often spent as much time doing odd jobs as working construction, yet in a very real sense, the oft-moved family was secure and solid. Just like those who had survived the Great Depression, their hardships had brought this Tucker generation closer together too. It had also given them a reason to work together to do whatever it took to escape their situation and life-style. Still, the promise of a bright future seemed as distant as the desert stars. And you could see a lot of stars in big sky country.

For anyone who isn't used to the vastness of Texas, the town of Seminole is a long way from Nashville or much of anywhere else. Lubbock and Midland are the nearest good-sized communities, and they are a healthy drive away. To the outsider or tourist Seminole would appear to be nothing more than a dusty little town sprinkled with a few thousand folks who get about as much shade from utility poles as they do from the trees.

Locals didn't notice it or comment on it, but outsiders
always wondered about the town's name. There seemed
to be almost a cruel irony in naming this dry, hot community for a Native American tribe that once roamed
through the swampy and wet Florida Everglades. Yet,
the Seminole tribe was tough and they could survive in
the roughest situations. To make a living in this part of
Texas a man or woman had to be tough and a survivor
too. So, in spirit if not in environment, there was a tie
between the city and its namesake. Certainly Beau
Tucker knew about toughness and survival.

Fall in Seminole is pretty much like every other season. Unlike the Northeast or Midwest, seasonal changes
here are subtle. The pace of life is slow, and the animal
life enjoys siestas as much as the local humans. The only
thing that disturbs the sameness of the passing moments
and really stirs things up are the storms which rumble
out of New Mexico and race along the flatlands. While
they don't last long, they do give the locals something to
talk about until the next one comes along. And that
makes a tornado something to look forward to almost as
much as something to fear.

With all that in mind, logic would seem to dictate that
Seminole would be a place that produced Medal of
Honor winners or world champion rodeo riders, not a
town that produced people who would change the
course of country music. The folks in this town were
mainly common people, bent on staying that way. The
night skies may have been clear and full of stars, but
stars walking on the streets, that seemed all but unthinkable.

Yet Larry Gatlin was born here. This is the place that
gave him something that served him well in Nashville,
New York and Los Angeles. So if lightning could strike
once, couldn't it hit twice? In Texas anything is possible,
or so people say.

On October 10, 1958, ten years after Larry Gatlin was

born, lightning did hit Seminole one more time. On that day Beau and Juanita Tucker welcomed their last child Tanya Denise. Knowing what we know now, it goes without saying that their lives would never be the same. Yet at that moment she was just another mouth to feed, another soul to love, another child to push the couple on to escape their nomadic life and somehow find their pot of gold at the end of some distant rainbow. And as they held this small child they had to be wondering . . .

Who is Tanya Tucker?

Chapter Two

Defining the Dream

*From that very first moment I just fully believed it.
I didn't have any doubts. I could just hear it in her
voice.*

—Beau Tucker

As was usually the case, the Tuckers' days in Seminole
were numbered. Before Tanya sang her first note the
family had packed up to move. In the early summer of
1959 they were on the road again as Beau looked for
work in the construction trade.

This constant movement, the continual uprooting, the
quick loss of friends and the insecurity of never knowing
just how long they were going to remain in a state, a
town or even a house, had to be tough on the family.
Many of today's child psychologists will point out that
this disruption—far removed from "normal" life—will
put children at risk in school and in handling interper-
sonal relationships throughout their lives. Yet in the
case of the Tucker family, the "hopscotching around the
country" life-style, pulling up stakes on a moment's notice and heading down the open highway, may have
been the best possible preparation for a career that was
beckoning them just around a few more bends.

Country music stars are modern day gypsies. They
bring their buses and a large family of workers into a
town for a day or two, set up shop, work with the locals,
and then, just as quickly, sever the ties and disappear to
reenact the entire scene at the next stop. The homes
where they spend most of the time have wheels, their

roots are somewhere in their past, and their dreams tend to follow the sun. Even when they do get to their real addresses, the ones with the brick walls and the grassy yards, the entertainers can't seem to spend more than a week or so relaxing before they are ready to hit the pavement again. These people appear to have a built-in wanderlust that keeps them traveling from city to city and date to date. This wanderlust is almost like a drug. They live for the road.

Barbara Mandrell began touring before she was a teen and she still understands the desire not to stay in one spot for too long. "I don't really like to work a week or two in the same place," Barbara admitted in 1994. "I want to be someplace different every night. I feel better and I am much more motivated when I am on the move." And when she is working, she is moving.

This need for movement, the desire for changing landscape, the comfort in setting up and breaking down might make a normal person crazy, but it is what keeps country music performers sane. If they don't have a bit of gypsy in their souls, then the life-style of 200 to 250 one-night-stands a year would eat them alive. They must have it in their blood to survive. Without it they will never be able to pay the price to be a star.

Tanya Tucker was literally born into that life-style. Her education in picking up and moving was absorbed in her DNA pattern before her real memories began. It was almost as if Beau had picked a job which would best prepare his daughter and their family for a life spent in a Silver Eagle bus. In Tanya's mind moving on was as natural as the sun rising in the morning. It was nothing to fear and something to look forward to. It was not *a* way of life, it was *the* way of life.

Something else which was very natural for this little girl was hearing country music. Her life was not filled with rock 'n' roll or Mother Goose, it was filled with steel guitars and fiddles. The small towns the Tucker family passed through in Texas, New Mexico, Arizona and Nevada were alive with the rural music of the people. So it was only natural that when the family was going down the road that the car radio was playing the songs of Hank Williams, Bob Wills or Patsy Cline. When a station was tuned in at home, Marty Robbins, Kitty Wells and Don Gibson were taking turns coming into the Tuckers' kitchen or living room. When the family visited a local fair or stock show, it was Nashville's bread and butter which offered the greatest entertainment thrill on the midway or under the big tent. In this dusty world, it was country music that provided the poetry that defined the people's lives, that explained their hardships. And the people who sang this music were the locals' heroes and role models. They were bigger stars than Clark Gable or Mickey Mantle.

The people of West Texas and eastern New Mexico were chest-thumping proud of Marty Robbins and Ernest Tubb. They talked about Bob Wills as if he were Babe Ruth. Hank Williams, who had died an alcoholic at twenty-nine, was spoken of in terms usually reserved for Bible figures. These simple folk forgave the country music stars their excesses and always took note of their genius. The personalities who sang on the radio and sold flower and headache powders along with their records, were as much a part of the fabric of their lives as their relatives, and in many cases, these men and women of song had far more influence. They were loved.

Country music had a loyal and sincere following. A country music fan would stay a fan as long as he or she drew breath, rarely listening to anything but country music. This was the kind of fan that Beau Tucker was.

Yet, thanks in large part to a new medium called television, as Tanya Tucker grew, there were musical influences other than country that crept in from time to time. LaCosta still talks about when she and Tanya sang along with the Lennon Sisters on "The Lawrence Welk Show." The older Tucker girl claims the first song Tanya ever learned was "Sad Moves" by the Lennon Sisters. Picturing Tanya on stage now with the Lennons at the Lawrence Welk Theater in Branson, Missouri, is a real leap of imagination, but back then she wanted to be just like them. Or at least she wanted to be on television. She didn't know what a spotlight was, but it was already reaching out to her.

Even at the age of two and three singing was something that took up a big part of Tanya's life. She sang to entertain herself. She sang when she was happy, when she was sad, when she was playing in the yard or going to sleep at night. She seemed to always be singing. Besides the Lennons, she learned tunes by Hank Williams, Patsy Cline and even Elvis Presley.

As her preschool years passed it was not unusual to catch the little girl, eyes sparkling and blond head shaking, standing in front of a mirror, using a hairbrush for a microphone and warbling at the top of her lungs. What might have shocked some who strolled by the Tucker home in the early days was that they never heard the little girl singing the strains of "London Bridge Is Falling Down" or "Row Row Row Your Boat." Tanya didn't sing children's songs. She didn't like them. She didn't think they were serious music. Tanya only sang the "real" stuff. When she cut loose, it was on "You Ain't Woman Enough To Take My Man," "Your Cheatin' Heart" and "I Fall To Pieces." In many cases she had no idea what the mournful lyrics of these ballads meant, but she must have somehow felt the songs' passion. When she sang them, she gave it all she had each and every time.

Prancing in front of a mirror is something that at one time or another almost every child does. Pretending is every healthy-minded child's best growth experience. Yet when Tanya was singing, it was different. To her this was no kid's fantasy. She seemed to take it a bit more seriously. She actually seemed to be working on styling and phrasing, and her movement seemed calculated to get attention. In her mind she wasn't in a bedroom, she was really on stage in front of thousands of screaming fans. Unlike most other children, there appeared to be a purpose behind her performance. Yet most of the folks around the house didn't notice. To them it was just a way to keep little sis out of their hair and occupied for a few moments, and they were thankful for the diversion. At times Tanya was a handful and a half.

Tanya had enough energy for two or three children. She was generally well-behaved, but full of life. She had spirit and spunk. At times she seemed almost hyper. Because she was always running, racing, jumping and climbing, her mother was thrilled that the little girl liked to spend so much time outside. This saved on the wear and tear this little dynamo left inside their home. There were times when she lamented the fact that she couldn't channel all that force in a more productive way. Yet Tanya was more than just perpetual movement and dynamic lungs.

Even as a first grader Tanya was generous, readily sharing her toys with classmates. Unlike many tomboys and children with an overabundance of energy, she was also gentle. She would pick up and hold a teddy bear or a kitten as if it were a fragile piece of china. But she could also throw a ball or swing a bat as hard as any boy. She was a delightful mixture of sugar and spice with a little cougar and wolf tossed in. She was unlike any other child anyone had ever seen.

Besides music, her love was horses. She had ridden for the first time at five and it was an experience that all but consumed her. In the southwest desert it was not uncommon for a little girl to grow up with a greater love for cowboys than Barbie dolls, and in Tanya's case the dolls finished a very poor second. When she wasn't singing, she talked about horses and riding all the time. Given an opportunity she would have ridden every hour of every day. She was Dale Evans in the saddle, except in her mind she was doing all the damage on the bad guys. She was not about to wait to be saved by the handsome cowhand. She was the one who was going to be doing the saving. This aggressive desire to win attitude, the "be the hero mind-set," the challenge-the-wind desire, made her father smile. This is the spirit he wanted for his child. It was what he thought of as the strongest facets of his own personality. He knew that it was hard to control, but it was so easy to challenge.

All he had to do to get Tanya to do or try almost anything was say, "I'll bet you can't do that." In her mind she *could* do anything. And even in the early years of grade school it was this inborn "do anything" attitude that set her apart from most other kids. The rarely smiling, impatient blonde was determined to set the standard for everyone else to follow. When she was first, it made her very happy. She seemed to live for it.

Yet not all of her days were a joy. She was by her own admission far from a perfect child. Being the youngest, even if she was the product of a poorer family, meant that she was spoiled. And spoiled children can be a handful even when they don't have a lot of spunk or energy. Tanya had both and a temper and stubborn streak to match.

She was at times willful, high-strung and almost impossible to control. In these ways she was also a lot like her father. It was often easier to go along with her than put her on a leash. Still there were things she did which couldn't be ignored. During those moments father and daughter clashed. And to their fights Tanya brought the same passion that she had when she sang in front of the mirror or rode horses. This meant that the discussions could be loud and sometimes drawn out. Beau would make his points and Tanya would make hers, but there was no doubt as to who was going to win. Yet that didn't mean that Tanya would give up easily. She fought until there was no fight left. In the end, after the punishment had been laid out, Tanya would hug her dad and tell him she loved him. Then she would go on as usual, until they crossed wires again.

Beau and Tanya were cut from the same mold, and Beau must have recognized it early. He knew that she had his strong points, and he also saw in her his own weaknesses. He didn't want to harness or corral the good stuff, but he had to reshape the temper into something more positive. He did that the only way he knew how.

From time to time Tanya was spanked by Beau. Yet this didn't defeat her attitude or break her spirit. It also didn't seem to diminish her love for her father. The strong discipline may have even pushed her into always trying to prove to him that she was worthy of being his daughter. This exercise all but became a passion for the little girl. In her eyes Daddy was the most important person in the world and the best man who had ever lived. This must have fueled her desire to stand apart from her older brother and sister. When she rode a horse, ran a race, or even drew a picture, she constantly hoped that Beau was looking on and approving of what he saw. First and foremost she seemed to want Daddy to proudly say, "Tanya's my girl."

Besides her secret and deep interest in singing and the constant relocating, Tanya's early life was pretty much normal. She went to Sunday school and vacation Bible school, rode bikes, played ball and adopted every stray dog she could find. Yet as she would later remember, even though she appeared to be just another child, she thought of herself as being much different from those around her.

Tanya didn't feel like she fitted in with either the poor, middle-class or rich kids. She thought of herself as an outcast. She really didn't think that the other kids liked her or cared to really know her. At home she was fun and happy, and enjoyed being around her mom and siblings, but outside the house she felt strangely different. She was a loner. She liked adults much better than kids her own age.

Tanya had been around older people her whole life. She had always been talked to as if she were an adult. She thought like an adult, reacted like an adult, and in many ways talked older than her years. She thought that many of the games the other kids played were juvenile. Their immature ways of thinking often mystified her. She couldn't understand why they didn't keep up with music charts and performers. Why did they want to waste their time playing with marbles or dolls? There was a big world to see out there, and they didn't seem to notice or care. Their thoughts never went beyond right now. They didn't seem to have dreams. Tanya simply couldn't relate to people who didn't dream and dream big.

"I have always been an adult," Tanya would later say to interviewers. "My childhood was not robbed [from me] because I had already outgrown those kind of things. I didn't want to play with dolls. I wanted to do adult things."

So while others were outside playing with their dolls or balls, Tanya had her own group of friends to play with, except that they were playing on the radio. Loretta Lynn, Elvis Presley, Jimmie Rodgers, Frank Sinatra, Connie Smith and Hank Williams were her confidants. They had the toys she wanted. They were expressing themselves in ways she understood. They either had lived or were living their dreams, and as the years went by, she dreamed more and more of joining them on stage.

After several moves the Tuckers ended up in the desert town of Wilcox, Arizona. Wilcox was known as the home of Republic Picture's "Arizona Cowboy" Rex Allen. Everyone in town was justifiably proud of this native son. He had made it big in the world of entertainment and he had reached stardom by glorifying the cowboy roots of which they were so proud. With Rex Allen and country music everywhere, this was the perfect place for little Tanya Tucker to call home.

Her love of singing now had turned to a bona fide passion. The shows in front of the mirror had become more elaborate. Her dreams at night now centered more on making records, doing tours and becoming a star than riding her bike. She could picture herself signing autographs. She could see herself on television. She even saw Elvis in the audience cheering her on as she performed one of his big hits. She dreamed of movies and cars and handsome men wooing her at every turn. Night after night she dreamed of the spotlight.

After a while all of these big dreams were too much for the little girl to keep inside of her. This nine-year-old had to share her desires of stardom. She was tired of standing in one place and singing just in front of a mirror. She had to tell someone about her visions—someone who would then see her talent and do whatever it took to get her an audition. In Tanya's young mind the only man who could make all her fantasies come true was her father. So one night when he came home from work she confidently approached him.

"I want to be a country singer," she announced.

Beau laughed for a moment and then with a smile added, "Sweetheart, you couldn't sing your way out of a paper sack."

"Can too!"

Even though he has spent years claiming he didn't know she could sing, it would have been just like Beau to have challenged Tanya by telling her she couldn't do something so that she would be forced to prove that she could. And if that was his strategy, it worked. As Beau sat in his chair and listened, Tanya stepped back and belted out a few notes. He was impressed. Nodding his head he indicated that she should continue. If he ever had any doubts about her talent, she won him over with her strong version of "Your Cheatin' Heart."

"From that very first moment I just fully believed it," Beau later said as he remembered back to that day. "I didn't have any doubts. I could just hear it in her voice."

Beau thought for a few days about his daughter's wishes. He considered if what he had heard was enough to push him to have others listen to Tanya. As he lay awake at night he mentally compared her to the others who were dominating the airwaves. In his mind she was as good as any of them. He had faith in those instincts too. After all, people had always said he had a knack for knowing what would and wouldn't make it in country music, and together he and Tanya could make it, he thought. After a few days Beau had fully convinced himself that he had finally found the ticket out of the dull and unsteady existence which had held them down for so long. The big time was just around the corner.

With Beau behind the wheel, Tanya began to perform at every talent show, beauty contest, fair and frog jumping contest within driving range of Wilcox. This proud father would talk until he was blue in the face to get her on a stage. No gathering was too small. He pushed and he prodded and again and again he won spots for his little girl. But he didn't stop with just finding her a place to sing.

Beau worked with Tanya too. He made her sing new material. When she was tired he forced her to practice longer and harder. He drove her to get better. He had her think about each song she sang and how to present it. And when she wanted to give up he would challenge her.

"Do you want to be a normal person or do you want to be a star?"

Tanya would always reply that she wanted to be a star. Then the hard sessions would continue.

Beau knew that everyone considered their nine-year-old daughters to have real stellar potential. So while he thought that Tanya's voice was better than any he had ever heard, he knew that he was going to have to polish her style and develop her poise before anyone who could make her a star would notice. And everything went to this goal. Nothing was simple anymore.

Beau had her read stories out loud to him. When she finished a story, he had her go back and read certain passages over again and again. Each time he urged her to do it with more feeling, more emotion. He wanted her to "feel" what she was reading. She had to "become" the part she was playing. She had to be the actress who was totally consumed by her part.

With the songs she sang it was the same way. When she sang their stories, she had to sell them. She had to feel each one's message and present it. It was this way both at home and in front of an audience. No half-hearted efforts would ever be accepted. When she was on stage Beau would watch the audience to see if they were buying into every word. He would note their reactions. Then after each show Tanya and Beau would review what he had seen and try to find ways to improve each phrase and movement.

In a very real sense Beau was his daughter's coach. He was the person who was working with her on the fundamentals of country music. Some might argue that she would have been better off with a voice teacher or a real manager, and while their case would normally be strong, this time Beau was the right person for the job. Tanya was young and raw, but she was also stubborn and strong beyond her years. She would have successfully fought off the suggestions of others. She would have broken other teachers. And while she often fought with Beau, because he was her father, she eventually listened and gave in to him. He could control her, others would have had a great deal more problems. To this day she and Beau have battles and disagreements, but Tanya believes that she would have never gotten started without him. She would have never made it without his pushing her all the way.

"Dad heard me singing and thought I might have some talent," Tanya matter-of-factly states. "I give him credit for that." And she also gives him credit for driving her to the shows, putting his schedule behind hers, and working with her for hours on developing her talent. From the day that she told him she wanted to be a country singer, Beau essentially gave up his life and gave it totally to Tanya. As she would later say, "I am his only hobby."

Looking back some might be amazed as just how many hours each day Beau invested in making sure his daughter was prepared for stardom—prepared to make good on her one chance when it came. But what would surprise them even more was that Tanya was then and is now not the least bit bitter about losing those hours of her childhood. As a matter of fact, her feelings have always run the other way.

In 1992 on a concert stop in Dallas, she told Diane Jennings of the *Dallas Morning News,* "I wish I'd started sooner . . . I was pissed because I didn't get started when I was nine."

She may have wanted to start earlier, but she couldn't have wanted to work any harder than she did over the next three years. She may have dreamed of being an overnight sensation, but it just wasn't meant to be. The script for her life was to be much different.

Chapter Three

The Quest for Stardom

I'm sure everybody in town thought Billy Sherrill was nuts for signing a thirteen-year-old girl.
　　　　　　　　　　　　　　　—Tanya Tucker

"*I* want to be a country singer."

With that simple declaration an eight-year-old Tanya Tucker changed life not only for her Nevada family, but for millions of country music fans. But it didn't come overnight. This Shirley Temple in cowboy boots would need to simmer for a few years before she really exploded.

With her father behind her, beside her, and even in front of her, Tanya met more and more people in the entertainment business. From radio station owners to the entertainment committee chairmen of the local women's clubs, Tanya met them all. Ever smiling, ever charming, she shook their hand and politely asked to be on their show. More often than not, it worked.

Like an old favorite record, Beau kept telling people, "I've got this girl who can really sing." And to prove it he kept taking Tanya to fairs and talent shows throughout the area. He put more miles on the Tucker car in a week than most people drove in a month. It paid off as Beau wrangled a spot for his little girl on stage with everyone from local country bands to little kids twirling batons. What he and his daughter had was really a circus minus the elephants and clowns, and it was an act that would have gotten old in a hurry if not for a few small glimmers of hope.

At the ripe old age of nine, after just a few months of climbing out in front of crowds, Tanya walked up to Mel Tillis. Tillis was headlining at a local county fair and in a hurry to get set up for his show. Still, he took the time to listen as Tanya told him she wanted to be a country singer. Mel has long been known as one of the nicest folks in the entertainment business. A topflight songwriter who had penned such hits as "Detroit City" and "Ruby Don't Take Your Love to Town," his wildly successful days as a performer were still a few years ahead. He was better known as a man who once sang lead for Bob Wills than as a headlining act. So the accommodations along his row of one-night stands were not yet first class and the work load was still strictly blue-collar. Other acts in similar positions would have signaled for someone to delicately escort the little girl to another part of the fairgrounds. But not Mel. Easygoing and laid-back, a father of daughters who were waiting for him at home, he seemed amused by the little fireball. Their conversation went something like this.

"So you can sing country music?"

"Yes, sir," came the sure response.

"Then let me hear you."

And backstage, with no accompaniment, she sang for Mel the way that she had for her father a few months before. The entertainer and the members of Statesiders band which had gathered around were impressed with the kid's version of "Your Cheatin' Heart." They didn't have to beg Tanya to do another number. Almost before they asked she jumped right in. She was selling herself hard and fast, and she had the confidence to back up her pitch.

After a few numbers the confident and diminutive blonde stated very matter-of-factly, "I'm going to be a country music singer."

"Is that all you sing?" someone asked.

"That is all I like," Tanya shot back. "I don't have much use for rock 'n' roll, unless it's Elvis. I like him a lot." Several heads nodded in approval.

Someone else pointed out that Elvis really was a country boy and everybody laughed. Mel meanwhile took a long look at Tanya, shrugged his shoulders and asked her to go get her father. That afternoon the two men got together and Tanya went over a few numbers with Mel's top-notch band. The young girl had never had an opportunity to work with musicians who were as good at the craft as the Statesiders and it would be a while before Tanya had a chance to work with any group this good again. So she treasured and enjoyed every minute of it. She also made sure they followed her, not the other way around!

That night as Mel introduced Tanya and she ran through a half-dozen country standards, she also enjoyed the warm applause the crowd sent back after each tune. For the struggling Tuckers, all watching with beaming smiles, this was the big time. Who cared that the crowd numbered in just the hundreds and that Mel Tillis had never hit any higher than #10 on the charts, the spotlight was on Tanya and for a brief moment they had all tasted stardom. They savored this taste and it drove them on with an ever greater zeal.

At the next fair it was brother Don who talked his way backstage. This time the featured act was aging country music veteran Ernest Tubb. Tubb and his Texas Troubadours had been roaming the country music backroads for more than half a century. He had scored his first #1 during World War II. Dozens of other hits had followed including "Walking the Floor Over You" and "Have You Ever Been Lonely." While his last big hit was the standard "Thanks a Lot" in 1963, his place in history had been assured when, two years later, he was elected to the Country Music Hall of Fame. Tubb was a much bigger personality that the then rising Tillis had been a few months before.

Tubb was also known as someone who could spot talent. Most gave him credit with plucking Loretta Lynn out of the shadows and putting her in the spotlight. His midnight radio show that aired on Nashville's WSM right after the Opry had served as a jumping-off point for a number of other future stars. A smart businessman who knew how to invest what he made, he was a country music legend with a truckful of high-powered contacts. In Don's mind this was the perfect man to hear his little sister. If Tubb liked her, then he might be able to provide a shortcut to Music City and fame. Don figured that the old country giant could make Tanya a star with one phone call. First, he had to hear the little girl.

Don talked the tall Texan into listening to Tanya. As Ernest listened, he smiled. She was good. He liked the real country sound he heard coming from the little girl. She sang with real passion. Impressed, Tubb offered her a chance to sing a standard on his show that night. Tanya walked into the spotlight, hit her number, received her applause and a fine compliment from the star, and left the stage. But if the Tuckers were hoping for any more than the spot and some encouragement, they didn't get it. Waving good-bye, Tubb hit the road with a friendly, "Good luck." This is what they probably should have expected.

The fact was that every night in every city Tubb was approached by scores of people who thought they had star potential and all they needed was a break. More often than not he would pick the best out and give them a chance at some local fame—an opportunity for Dad or Mom to take their picture onstage with him and his band, but that was generally it. This night would be no different.

Yet despite the disappointment of not having the Hall of Famer offer to introduce them to the powers at

Decca records, this evening must have been a real thrill for Beau. Ernest Tubb had been one of his favorites. This was the man whom Beau would imitate for his friends. In Beau's and almost all the other old-timers' minds, this was a star of mammoth proportions, a real headliner who walked the stage of the mother church of country music each and every Saturday night. Tubb had introduced Lefty Frizzell, Hank Thompson, Kitty Wells, Hank Williams, Patsy Cline and so many others. And now he was introducing "Little Miss Tanya Tucker." That meant that his daughter was in some pretty good company and he could brag that Tanya had shared a stage with the likes of a country music giant. This might prove to open a bunch of doors.

Appearances with the likes of Tillis and Tubb drove Tanya and her family forward. Judging on the success they had already experienced, this business must not have looked too hard. Just around the corner had to be that pot of gold. All they had to do was put in a few more weeks or months and then it would all come together. Yet in this case appearances were deceiving.

In 1969 the Tucker family left Wilcox and Rex Allen country and moved to Phoenix. The bigger city seemed to offer more chances for Tanya to gain more exposure. There were talent shows everywhere and Beau made sure that Tanya entered practically all of them. Much to the amazement of her father, she didn't win a single one. She was beaten out by everything from small kids dancing in circles to old ladies' quartets. Still Beau continued to take her back because he felt that there was something in her voice that "just sounded right." He couldn't understand why no one else in the area picked up on it.

Between jobs and frustrated with the local offerings, Beau determined that Tanya was seasoned enough for Nashville. In his mind the Phoenix folks simply couldn't recognize real commercial talent, the kind that people paid high dollar to see. Local talent shows were just places where the cutest kid often doing the most bizarre thing won. Tanya shouldn't be billed with tap dancers and classical piano pounders; she should be on stage with Loretta Lynn.

With this in mind, Beau poised himself and Tanya to make the big jump. With his break from his construction work destined to last a few weeks, he planned a trip across half the country to Nashville, Tennessee. He did so knowing that he had no contacts, no references, and no real hope of meeting the right people. What he did have was the simple faith in his daughter's abilities, his own instincts, and a new Cadillac.

He had purchased the fancy car even though he knew that he couldn't really afford it. He had done it for the sake of making an impression. He had to convince the Music City people that he and his daughter were not hicks. He wanted them to judge them on Tanya's talent. He felt the best way to accomplish this was to give the impression of having already made it back home. The Caddy may not have turned many heads in Nashville, but it sure was a comfortable way to get there and back.

Looking back on that first junket to the big time, Tanya understands why they took the chance on the trip. "He had big dreams, and I had big dreams too." Yet most times dreams aren't enough.

Armed with a suitcase full of clothes and a home-made demo tape of very poor quality, Beau and Tanya took off to Nashville. With Tanya in her Sunday best, they knocked on doors all up and down music row. After a great deal of rejection, they finally got invited to see Danny Davis.

Davis was one of Nashville's more unique fish. He was a Massachusetts born trumpet player who had ended up in Music City. Educated at the New England Conservatory of Music, he had played in bands with the likes of Gene Krupa, Bob Crosby and Sammy Kaye be-

fore coming to Nashville and working in production at
RCA for Chet Atkins. His soon to be highly successful
Nashville Brass band was just a year old, and at this time
he was not well-known outside the cradle of the recording industry.

None of that bothered Beau. He had someone who
would listen and with the zeal of a revival preacher he
spouted out countless words of praise for his daughter.
Davis listened, talked to the girl, checked out the tape
and finally observed, "I think she is going to be a whiz."
While that sounded good, he then offered them no
more help. As the two left, any passerby could have seen
their fallen faces and probably guessed what had happened.

Tanya would later say that she felt that Davis and
RCA wanted to sign her. They liked what they saw and
what they heard. Yet there was something holding them
back.

"I think they wanted me," Tanya stated, recalling
meeting the recording giant. "I just don't think they
knew what to do with a nine-year-old girl." RCA doesn't
recall the story the same way, but they would agree with
the latter. What do you do with a nine-year-old girl in
country music?

Davis had spoken the only real encouraging words
that Tanya and Beau received. Most people didn't even
have time to listen to the tapes. Doors closed faster than
they opened. Things got so bad that Beau even played
the tape and talked about Tanya with a record store
owner. After listening to the music the owner told Beau
he wouldn't put a penny against fifty thousand dollars
that the little girl would ever be a star. The self-labeled
expert reckoned that it would "be a waste of a penny."

Those like Davis who took the time to give Beau the
opportunity to give his sales speech and Tanya a chance
to perform couldn't have helped being a little impressed. She did have style and talent, and beyond that

her poise and voice were years ahead of her physical age. But country music had never had a place for children. Brenda Lee and others had been pushed toward rock 'n' roll. Music city labels and producers didn't look for music that would appeal to teenagers. It wasn't their market. If Tanya had been singing about bubble gum or teenage crushes, she might have gotten them interested in trying her in pop. As it was the little girl was raising her voice in tributes to drinking, cheating and loneliness. Even if they had opted to try and record Tanya, who can blame them for feeling that they couldn't market those recordings. Who would have believed it?

Another of the things that may have worked against Tanya and Beau was the relationship between the singer and manager. Nashville tended to shy away from acts where the father was the person making the business decisions. The fact was that stage parents, even those with adult children for clients, had an even worse name in Music City than they did in Los Angeles. At that time, the one exception seemed to be Irby Mandrell. He was able to work with CEOs and bookers because he had been linked to the music industry first as a performer, second as a music store operator and finally as a friend of country music personalities such as Joe Maphis, Johnny Horton and Patsy Cline. In that sense Irby was seen as an insider and was rarely thought of as a stage father. Beau was not an insider and in reality he was a stage father. He had no hobbies except his daughter. If was fair for people to question whether his quest to bring Tanya what she said she really wanted was already consuming his own judgment. What sane man would listen to a kid?

While the week in Nashville was largely a bust, the two did get to take in The Grand Ole Opry. Most folks who had been shut out of as many offices as they had might have viewed the performance in a bittersweet fashion. Rather than sadly looking on in a defeated and

demoralized fashion, Beau and Tanya watched the legends perform while measuring the talent against their
own. And while they respected every act they saw, they
weren't intimidated. They still believed that they belonged on stage with them. They left town even more
sure of that than when they came. If this trip was meant
to test the resolve and belief in what they were doing,
then they had passed that test with flying colors.

Back in Phoenix Beau didn't let the grass grow under
his feet. Calling on the phone and knocking on every
door he could find, he managed to wrangle Tanya a spot
on a local television program. "The Lew King Show"
was a kids' show but it did have an audience and Tanya
needed exposure. For a while Tanya was a regular on a
show that reached kids her age and younger. The girl
who had tried to wow Nashville and had won over Mel
Tillis didn't take to the fact that she was trying to reach
out and touch children who had just gotten out of
diapers. She hated singing songs like "How Much Is
That Doggie in the Window," and certainly such tunes
were not allowing her to show the passion and raw edge
that made her voice unique. To the young entertainer
"The Lew King Show" was like marking time. Both she
and her father knew there had to be something better
out there for her.

By mid-1970 Tanya had left children's television behind as the Tucker clan moved to Little Rock, Arkansas,
while Beau tied up some lose ends in the west. Their
address was ironically the Watergate Apartments. The
Ozarks didn't offer much hope, so from the "Land of
Opportunity" they journeyed to the Rocky Mountains.
It was in Saint George, Utah, that the Tuckers landed,
following Beau to a new construction site. Out in the
middle of "entertainment nowhere" Beau and Tanya
had to wonder if this move spelled doom for their
dream. Yet they didn't have to look too far for a certain
kind of inspiration. In Provo a local family called the

Osmonds were beginning to make a splash by spotlighting their own children singing and dancing. Andy Williams had put them on national television. Adults and kids were responding to their music. Maybe there was hope of finding someone who would listen and like what they heard and do the same for them.

Once again they looked for and found local talent shows and fairs. It was becoming easier and easier to get Tanya on the bill, she was that good. The problem was that she just wasn't heard by the right people. On a lark Beau drove the family on a three-hundred-mile trip back to Phoenix to the Arizona State Fair to attempt to change the demographics of Tanya's audience. At the big fair, Judy Lynn, a thirty-six-year-old Idaho native who had landed on the country charts three times in the early sixties, was on the entertainment bill. Maybe somehow Tanya could meet Judy and sing in front of a really big audience. It was a long shot, but Beau was used to that. In his mind it was worth both the time and effort.

Judy Lynn was not on the edge of stardom. She was just a moderately successful act whose only top ten record had been "Footsteps of a Fool." That title seemed appropriate as she allowed Tanya's brother Don to visit her backstage before the show and then talk her into listening to his little eleven-year-old sister sing. She had probably been swayed by the fact that two of country music's biggest superstars had shared their stages with Tanya. But if she was moved by Tubb and Tillis's acceptance of Tanya, that fact only served to open the door. Tanya's talent would be the ticket that got her on stage.

Just like Mel and Ernest, Judy liked what she heard. Her band did too and they agreed to let Tanya sing a few numbers for their state fair audience. Tanya was on that night. She had more poise and charisma than she had ever before exhibited. She seemed to feed off every cheer. She and the crowd got into a grove that set off flashbulbs and eventually brought the audience to its feet on several occasions. After that response, after the thrill of signing a few autographs, it was no wonder that the Tuckers drove back to Utah with a feeling of an impending upswing in their fortunes. It didn't turn out that way. A year later they were right where they were before the fair, doing small local gigs and talent shows. What they didn't know was that the long drive to and from Arizona would pay off in time, but right now it appeared just to be another false start.

Tanya's next taste of show business came not from Nashville and country music but from Hollywood and the movies. Robert Redford has picked the area around Saint George, Utah, to film his new movie, *Jeremiah Johnson*. The script had Redford playing the real-life mountain man Johnson in a plot that was a good dose of fiction mixed up with a bit of fact. Any motion picture that asked ticket buyers to believe that Hollywood's most handsome leading man was portraying one of history's ugliest known characters was asking for a huge leap of faith. Nevertheless, hungry theater patrons of the time were more than ready to go to any film in which Redford appeared, no matter how many liberties were taken with actual history.

Like everyone else in the region, the Tucker family was interested in what was taking place just outside of town. Led by Juanita, Tanya roamed up to the location shooting and watched with great interest as the cast and company went through the various shots. It was during one of the breaks that Juanita mentioned to the director that her daughter was the young lady riding a horse just across the way. He studied the girl and her mount for a few moments and then remarked, "I sure could use that horse."

Tanya was not pleased with the thought of having someone else riding one of the few special things she owned. So she balked at the invitation. After a few minutes of discussion, the director and the child came to a compromise; he got the horse for the next day's shooting, but Tanya would do the riding. Though only as an extra, this marked Tanya's first stint on film. Later she could laughingly take credit for Redford's and the film's big box office success.

The movie was fun. It was a pleasant diversion from the hard practice sessions her father was putting her through. At twelve, Tanya was beginning to wonder if all the work and effort was really worth it. No one had taken much interest in her in months. Her career was stuck in the mud. Maybe the big dreams she had dreamed weren't really going to become reality. What was the use in working without any immediate rewards?

Perhaps Tanya's future and her stardom hung on a school night in Utah, and maybe it didn't. But the impression that one evening made would long be remembered by Tanya and her family. She and Beau had been working on several new songs for what seemed to the small girl a very long time. She was tired, she was frustrated, and she didn't want to learn anymore. When he asked her to do them again, she rebelled.

"It's late and I've got homework."

"If you don't finish this you can go out and hoe weeds in the yard!"

"But . . ."

"No buts . . ."

Tanya could see that there was no use arguing with her father. He had his mind made up. When she did her best on the new material, she could do her homework and go to bed. Yet this time she didn't want to give in. So rather than go through the songs again, she charged outside. Finding a hoe, she spent the next hour alone in the dark digging in the yard. As time dragged by and the songs of the night began filling the air, Tanya must have glanced back toward the door hoping to see her father waving her in. Yet he didn't come to the door. Stubbornly, in spite of being a bit frightened, she continued to dig. Finally, sometime before midnight, she decided that Beau was even more stubborn than she was. Swallowing her pride, she tossed the hoe down and marched back to the house. Launching back into the material, she didn't quit singing until she had mastered Beau's newest bit for her show, "Every Fool Has a Rainbow."

Somehow that song must have seemed strangely appropriate during this period of time. For almost three years they had chased rainbows over a third of the United States and all they had to show for it were bald tires and dusty memories. Many who knew them believed that they had to be stupid to continue pushing on. Why didn't they just give up?

It was a question that even Beau couldn't answer with anything more than, "She has just got something special." And that answer failed to convince the doubters. He was wasting his time trying to make a star out of a little girl. They also thought he was stealing Tanya's chance at being a little girl.

All things considered, the Tuckers were happy in Utah. They wished for more success, but the beauty of the countryside and the people who had become their friends gave them a warm feeling for Saint George. If their dreams had been different, if Beau hadn't believed so much in Tanya, these gypsies might have even stayed. Tanya herself would often say that no one in the family wanted to leave Utah, but Beau thought they had to move to get his youngest closer to the spotlights and the "connected" people in the world of entertainment. This move from Utah would therefore become the first of several moves that the family made based solely on what their youngest daughter wanted.

Like the Okies in the Great Depression who got on Route 66 and headed west looking for work, Beau Tucker followed the old legendary highway too. Only he stopped in Las Vegas, the world's entertainment capital.

In attitude and moral climate, Vegas was about as far
from Saint George as a man could get. In 1970 hookers
would often walk the streets and try to flag down cars.
Slot machines were everywhere, including the rest
rooms. Dancing topless was a respected form of employment, and having a few drinks with breakfast was
not frowned upon. The mob's biggest bosses came to
town and rubbed elbows with casino owners. And when
Elvis flew in, the whole place stopped dead. No place in
America, or for that matter the world, was like Vegas,
and few places wanted to be like the city that never
slept.

Five miles south of the "Strip" a sign read HENDERSON-
BOULDER DAM. Ten miles down that straight road was the
small bedroom community of Henderson. When the
Tuckers moved there the town's main point of interest
was a long, black, smoke-belching chemical plant. Those
who didn't drive to Vegas found work here. And most of
them, like Beau's family, resided in one of hundreds of
cookie cutter mobile homes.

Henderson was a tribute to the American postwar
years. It looked like it had been the result of planning,
not imagination. The blocks were square and precisely
laid out. The homes all seemed to look alike. And
trailer parks, with their small yards and hot tin roofs,
gave testament to just how quickly the area had grown
up.

The Tuckers lived in a double-wide mobile home,
complete with a green metal canopy for a garage and a
small plot of sparse desert grass out front that was
called a yard. Within a few weeks of their arrival, Tanya
had turned the area into a home for an ever growing
number of stray dogs. It was typical of what life was for
most families in the area. It was their security and the
answer to their small dreams. For the Tuckers it was a
stopping-off point along the path to a much bigger goal.

For the first time in his married life Beau was uninterested in finding a great job for himself. He was working hard, but not to raise money for his own dreams. He was pushing to make enough money to really fund Tanya's shove into the big time. After a short while, frustration took its toll. He wasn't able to keep enough of what he was earning. The family's living expenses ate too much of what he made. He couldn't save enough. He knew that he needed at least $1,100 to book Tanya in for a semiprofessional demo session. Try as he would he simply couldn't put that kind of bankroll together. Something was always getting in the way—mainly bills.

Without the sessions, he didn't have much chance at getting any real professional booker or manager to listen to Tanya. His old tapes simply were too ragged, too homemade sounding to best present the fairly polished performer into which Tanya had grown.

Beau had tried working hard and praying hard and neither had paid off. In most places those two options were the only thing open short of armed robbery that a man could use. Yet in Vegas there was one other way to go, and Beau, whose whole life had been a gamble decided to try it.

Taking what little money he had scraped together, Beau stoked up on coffee and spent two nights at the keno tables. As if scripted for a Hollywood movie, he won $1,100. Quitting when he had the barest minimum needed for his dreams, he walked away. A few days later he booked time at United Recordings. Using names given to him by friends and acquaintances, he literally roamed the streets finding musicians who were looking for gigs. When he had located enough of them, he drove to the studio.

The group that Beau had assembled for those few hours of work were ragged at best. Never would this motley group have been solid enough to tour with, but this was still a big jump from the homemade tapes he and Tanya had made with no help.

With the clock running and hardly any time devoted for rehearsal, the songs he and Tanya had been forced to pick out were bland, standard offerings. There was nothing original in the group, but Beau didn't think the numbers themselves had to be original. After all, he had a very original singer singing them.

In three hours Tanya cut six songs. The best of the lot seemed to be "Put Your Hand in the Hand" and "For the Good Times." None, not even these sharpest two, were good enough to stand up in any kind of release. Yet there was something special on this tape. Maybe it would get Beau the break he needed.

Back at home he put together mailings to all the area talent scouts. Some called back, but not one of these offered any quick work. Some called and offered work if Beau would pay them money up-front. Beau saw right through these scam artists and moved on. After a few weeks, Beau was getting desperate. On a tip he contacted a local songwriter. She had penned stuff that Elvis had recorded and she had dabbled in the agent and representation game. Like his two nights at the table, this gamble paid off.

Dorris Fuller had represented several big stars including Johnny Rivers. Her reputation was solid. She was also honest. Dorris listened to the tapes and contacted Beau. She told him that the kid had something. She said that she knew it from the moment she heard the child's voice. She wondered if Beau would mind if she sent the tapes to a friend in Nashville. Beau's answer was a loud affirmation of what Dorris already knew.

Fuller's Nashville friend was the already legendary record producer Billy Sherrill. Sherrill was known as a star-maker. He had been behind many of Music City's biggest acts and records. When he received Dorris's letter and listened to the tapes, he couldn't believe that this voice belonged to a girl just approaching her teen years. Impressed, the man who had produced such hot properties as Loretta Lynn and Tammy Wynette, cleared his schedule and made a special trip to Las Vegas to hear Tanya in person. Once there he was even more moved. He promised the Tuckers a recording contract and then returned home to pick out material and set up a session.

After years of waiting and working, it was now coming almost too quickly. Tanya's bike and her dogs took a backseat to the most intense practicing she had ever known. This time she didn't mind at all. She was going back to Nashville and there would be no doors on which to knock because they already had a key in their hands. Still Tanya knew the risk that Sherrill was taking. Remembering Nashville's reaction from a few years before she told her family, "I'm sure everybody in town thinks Billy Sherrill is nuts for signing a thirteen-year-old girl." Nuts or not, he was going to give her a shot.

As excited as Tanya was, Beau must have been feeling a great sense of relief. His three-year gamble had paid off. He had found his ticket and recognized its potential. He had successfully banked his one chance at escaping the life of a common man. One could never imagine the emotion that must have been continually flooding his heart in those days. No longer did he look like the world's biggest fool.

A month after they met Sherrill for the first time, Billy had Tanya and Beau in Nashville at Columbia's Studio C. With the city's finest pickers behind her, the producer presented to the girl a song he knew was going to be a big hit. She took a listen and then strongly, but politely, turned down Al Gallico's "Happiest Girl in the U.S.A."

Years later Sherrill would deny that this was the first song he presented to his soon to be teen sensation. "I never pitched it to Tanya," Sherrill would claim scores of times. "From the first I wanted a grown-up girl sound because of her grown-up voice."

Despite Sherrill's denials, Tanya is convincing in her memories of that day. "Billy knows it happened because Al Gallico came in and had the song with him and it was already a record."

Tanya remembers listening and saying, "That's just not my song, Billy."

She then claims that Sherrill turned to the songwriter and said, "You heard what she said, Al. There is nothing I can do."

Whatever the real story is, whether Sherrill pitched and Tanya balked or not, the next tune the producer had in mind was going to get rave reviews all around. A few days before the session Sherrill had been watching "The Tonight Show with Johnny Carson." A pop singer named Bette Midler had touched a bit of magic with an Alex Harvey song entitled "Delta Dawn." It was a story song, one that the producer felt would work in favor of Tanya's young age. It would allow her to show off her mature voice without having to be too mature herself.

When it was first played for her, Tanya didn't like the tune much. But Billy insisted and had her listen again. As she began to grow used to it, the melody and words got stuck in her mind. It wasn't "Don't Come Home a Drinkin'," but it was catchy. So without too much fussing, she agreed to lay down the tracks. Sherrill knew he had a hit when everyone left the studio that day still humming that first song.

For the Tuckers it was out of the session and back to Henderson. For the first time in years Tanya's fate was out of their hands. Now it was up to Columbia and the company's most famous producer. As the hot desert sun looked down on a small energetic blond girl riding a bike in the sand, the days and weeks slowly passed by. It was as bad as waiting for Christmas, but the result would have them all believing in Santa again. After a three-year false start, Tanya was about to be a star!

Chapter Four

Delta Dawning

Tanya Tucker is one of my favorite singers, and one of the most unique country singers to come along in a very long time.

—Kitty Wells

*O*ne year before Tanya Tucker was born the Decca label signed a thirteen-year-old girl to a recording contract. Her name was Brenda Lee and she became known as "Little Miss Dynamite."

Brenda hit the country charts for the first time in May of 1957 with a song entitled "One Step At a Time." The number climbed the charts for almost three months before landing in the top twenty.

When Tanya's "Delta Dawn" was released the comparisons between Tucker and Lee immediately began, and there were a great many similarities. Both kids were seasoned pros who had appeared on countless talent shows before they were signed to record. Both had been featured on local television shows. Both had worked on stage with legends before they had been recorded. In Brenda's case the list was a long one which included Elvis Presley. Both had a real flair for showmanship on stage. And public relations agents claimed that while they both sang "big people" songs, that they were still "little girls" at heart.

Yet the most obvious comparison was the one made about their voices. Like Brenda, Tanya had a full-grown voice. Like Brenda, Tanya had a style and sound that was all her own. Like Brenda, anyone who listened to her once would always be able to recognize her again no matter what song she was performing. And like Brenda, she sounded like no one else in Nashville.

Brenda Lee's first jump onto the country charts in 1957 was her last appearance on that chart for more than twelve years. Little Miss Dynamite didn't go away, she simply exploded on the rock 'n' roll side of the ledger. Over the next decade she landed in the top forty twenty-eight times. Eleven of those hits went top ten. "I'm Sorry" became not only her signature song, but one of rock music's classics. *Life* magazine reported that she was this country's youngest female self-made millionaire. And a lot of this happened before she learned to drive a car!

Tanya probably didn't know a great deal about Brenda Lee's youthful success until the press jumped into the comparisons, but she and Beau couldn't have minded. After all, if Tanya's career course held as well as Miss Lee's, there were some mighty good times ahead. Brenda had a long list of hits and had earned a healthy amount of cash during the years before she turned twenty. Yet, in a way, the Tuckers had a tougher road up the steep trails of "Success Mountain."

Brenda might have made her first appearance on the charts in country, but she quickly gravitated over to rock 'n' roll. In the 1950s and 1960s the rock industry and public relations machines not only knew what to do with a child act, they welcomed kids and wrote songs for them. Back in the present, Tanya was recording in Nashville, singing country songs and had no immediate plans to jump across the chart barrier. Country didn't have a record of working with youthful voices and acts, they didn't write songs for kids, and in the past they had never really made room for them. If they were instrument playing whizzes, they found a place in the band for them, but a singer? A thirteen-year-old fronting for her own band was unheard of. So while Brenda Lee had been heading down a road well-traveled, Tanya Tucker was blazing a new trail.

For some folks blazing a new trail might have been scary—kind of a "hillbilly" junket to the "Twilight Zone." Yet Beau had been walking to his own drummer for years, and certainly Tanya was not a typical example of a thirteen-year-old. What was most in their favor was that neither of them were odds players, and neither cared much what other people thought. They were bound and determined to make it to the top and if anyone told them they couldn't, then they weren't going to listen. They believed in Tanya's talent and her dream to that great an extent.

So it was no surprise that Tanya knew she had cut a hit in Nashville. She and her father weren't worried about the song or what the song would do on the charts. They were much too busy planning on putting together a band and a stage show and touring the nation to be concerned about anything like numbers and critical reviews. Who cared what others thought, up until now the experts had all been wrong anyway. The father and daughter were confident and they had faith that country music fans would buy into the "little girl with the big voice" now that they were finally being exposed to her. In their minds, there were no questions left to answer except how quickly can we get on with the show.

Their faith was rewarded in a big way. "Delta Dawn" was released in the spring of 1972, broke onto charts at #70 on May 13, 1972, and kept climbing through the various numbers until it jumped into the top ten. "Dawn" peaked on Billboard at #6. The song spent seventeen weeks on that Billboard chart. On other charts the song would continue to move up until it hit #1. Outside of country music they noted the song as well. It was a hit of career making and/or breaking proportions.

How big was it? On her very first release Tanya

crossed over the wide river between country and rock. Her version of "Delta Dawn" landed at #75 on the stations playing "that other kind of music." Less than a year later the tune would resurface and become a #1 pop hit for Helen Reddy. It would be Reddy's signature song for a couple of years until the release of "I Am Woman," but the truth was that Helen didn't sell the story like Tanya had. Long after country and rock fans had largely forgotten Reddy's "Dawn," Tanya would still be closing shows with it.

It had all happened with such rapidity. From nowhere to everywhere in the blink of an eye. From having no one know who Tanya Tucker was, to being recognized by just her first name. Much faster than almost any Nashville star since Connie Smith, Tanya was riding the top crest of a wave. Suddenly the press wanted to talk with her. Suddenly the record label had a need for thousands of publicity photos for immediate release. Suddenly the little girl had become Cinderella. And it had all happened—suddenly!

A lot of the curiosity might have been caused because so many thought that they had better strike fast because this little girl would no doubt become one of country music's quick disappearing acts. A majority of the press simply couldn't conceive of a kid lasting more than a year or so on the country music circuit. After that she would quickly begin fading back to high school dances, or in this case junior high dances, and church socials. Then she would disappear altogether. Yet for right now —at this moment—she was "the" story in country music.

When the writers met Tanya for the first time they got exactly what they must have expected from a very young girl. Her "little lady" qualities immediately won over the press and served to quickly disarm them. She was a slender, ash-blonde whose eyes appeared to be filled with fawnlike innocence. She had a quick friendly smile, a rapid-fire sense of humor and a childlike charm. She was very much like the cute puppy that always seemed to be looking out the window of a pet shop—so cute and helpless that you want to take her in your arms and protect her. And that is what they did; the media adopted this little star.

While she won the press over with her childlike qualities, what kept them asking questions were her adultlike responses. She may have been pictured riding her bike or playing with her dog, but she spoke of charts, performing and songs like an adult. She was cute like a little kitten, but she was also sly like a fox. She used charm to set her trap, then sprang it with brains. The reporters all walked away from the interviews writing stories that read the way Tanya wanted them to. Rarely did the writers realize just how crafty the girl was in the way she used them to develop the image and interest that would help sustain her past the year most had given her.

With good press and a great deal of interest, what Tanya and Beau both knew she needed was a follow-up hit to go with "Dawn." She got that when Sherrill tapped "Love's the Answer" as the second release. Capitol released it with a "B" side that sounded a great deal like "Delta Dawn." Almost immediately the disc jockeys began playing the secondary side and "Jamestown Ferry" was heard on the country airwaves almost as frequently as the "A" side. Because no one really knew which song was the real hit, beginning in late 1972 they both climbed the charts. They ended up topping out one place higher than "Dawn" at #5. Their chart ride was a very solid fifteen weeks. It was a very important statement for Tanya's career. It presented her as something other than a "one-hit sensation." She had already passed the likes of Jeannie C. Riley, who had scored once and taken it to the barn.

With the double-sided hit, a very rare commodity in country music, Sherrill knew that he had guessed right about the bright teenager. She was a rare bird, a combination child-adult—a very large voice in a rather small package. But that was just the beginning, the producer already knew her to be a great deal more too. She had more spunk and fire than 90 percent of the adult acts he had produced. And more importantly, between her and her father there was enough drive and unbridled energy to push a long freight train. "Yes," he told everyone, "this girl is special." And you could tell when he said it, the producer believed it!

Less than a year after rising from out of nowhere, Tanya made her first grab for the really big time. She received two Grammy nominations. The first was for her stirring rendition of what was to become a country classic, "Delta Dawn." The second was for Country Female Singer of the Year. She wouldn't win either award, but the recognition proved that she was being studied and observed well beyond Music City's inner circles. She was a name and she was definitely on her way to even bigger things. There were a lot of twenty-plus women in the business who were jealous.

In 1972 after releasing only two singles, "Delta Dawn" and "Jamestown Ferry," Tanya felt like she was ready to put her whole life in perspective. She told *Country Music* magazine, "It's taken me a long time to get where I am today. I made my first appearance at nine and I have been singing at beauty pageants and state fairs ever since."

A long time? Some who had labored twenty years before they had found any kind of success found it ironic that Tanya would think that four years was a long time to wait for a shot at the big time. Yet what they forgot to consider was that it was a third of her life. To a child four years was a lifetime. And in her mind, she had worked as hard as any female artist.

During the initial stages of her sudden career boost, Tanya spent most of her time doing guest shots on country music bills or rehearsing. Playing little girl games, something she never had much use for, was now a thing of the past. Her career was now everything. What spare time she did have was spent in Morgan Hill, California, on a cutting horse ranch. It was there that she met a young man with a sparkle in his eye and a hat on his head. He stole her heart from day one and he may have been the reason she still has a soft spot for cowboys. Yet when push came to shove it was the horses, not the cowboys, which would hold her attention the longest.

Morgan Hill's world famous cutting horses fascinated her. From the first day she walked onto the ranch she begged the ranch hands to let her work with the cattle. Once she sneaked off and tried it on her own and managed to start a minor stampede. It took several hours to round up the strays. Yet rather than get angry, it was this kind of desire which forced the cowboys to take a second look at the little wisp of a girl. Putting her on a mount, they showed her the basics. In no time she was cutting cows like a pro. She and her mount had become as one. Just like when she was on a stage, she was a natural. Within a week of getting her first cutting horse ride, she won third place at a cutting horse contest. To all those around her, it seemed that Tanya won at everything she tried.

As his little girl's success continued to build, Beau began to get more attention too. In most cases stage door parents push their children into acting or performance because of their own unfulfilled desire to be stars. These parents crave attention and yet rarely receive anything more than hostile glares from the media. They are painted as leeches and slave drivers and in many cases rightfully so. They are rarely respected or admired.

In Beau Tucker's case things were much different. He was pushing Tanya's career because she had asked— almost begged him to. He didn't want to be on stage, in the spotlight or in the news. He was a simple man who only wanted to be proud of his little girl. He didn't much care for cameras or reporters. Yet because of Tanya's mature poise, confident nature and charm, he was constantly sought out. Press, fans, and even adult performers wanted to know just what it was that he had that had enabled him to raise such a wonderful, bright kid. What were his secrets?

Uncomfortable in the spotlight, Beau would somewhat modestly tell people that his success as a father was due to, "Understanding and love for the child. You can't fight 'em, you have to fight for them. You have to listen too. I listen. My children proved a lot of times that I'm wrong. I even ask them from time to time what is wrong with me?" It was an honest approach that had so far served him and his kids very well.

To prove the listening point, he was originally wrong about Tanya's voice. A couple of major chart-busters had proved that. But he admitted it and went to work for her when she proved him wrong. In spite of the fact that going to bat for his daughter had cost him in a big way. For three years he couldn't get anyone besides his family to realize the little girl had real star potential. He also couldn't get consistent work. Still, he ignored the hardship and ridicule and kept fighting for his kid. Beau really was a man who lived what he stated. He was also someone who wouldn't take sole credit for putting Tanya into the big time.

First and foremost Beau would deflect the praise people sent his way back on Tanya. He wanted the press to know that his daughter was the one with the talent, he was just the old guy who ran a few errands for her. But he didn't stop there. He pointed out the faith and risks of Billy Sherrill and Capitol Records. He also thanked those who had helped them along the way. He never forgot Judy Lynn or Mel or Ernest. Then Beau would give credit to not only his wife, but his other two children. He made sure the press and public knew that he was as proud of them as he was of Tanya and that her career was a family deal, not just one little girl doing it all on her own.

It was from Beau's giving credit where credit was due that the press and fans very quickly learned that while Beau was manager and Tanya was the performer, everyone was involved too. Don, who had talked Tanya onto a host of stages when she was a complete unknown, had become her road manager. LaCosta had grown into the role of her little sister's assistant, tutor, playmate and buffer. She was there to do whatever it took to make sure that the homework got done, the songs were learned, that everyone was on time and that little sister was prepared for every appearance and every interview. Juanita was the cook, the secretary and the costume designer and maker. It was a family affair. It couldn't have worked any other way.

Whenever asked about her family's involvement in her career, Tanya would smile and proudly say, "I work for my family." And knowing what was going on behind the scenes she could have just as easily added, "and the family works for me."

And with two hits in the bank, that family was making plans to move away from Arizona and really hit the big time. They had a chance at going some place special and they weren't going to let this precious opportunity slide by. They were tired of the lack of security and they were tired of constant movement and eternal searching for a greener piece of grass and a brighter rainbow. They wanted a home, money in the bank and a chance at a sure future. It had been a long haul to this point, especially for Beau and Juanita; now they could see the light at the end of the tunnel.

Nashville and the long ribbon of concrete known as "the road" were just around the corner. Tanya was about to become country music's youngest superstar. The Tuckers were ready!

Chapter Five

On The Road

*She gives everything she's got. I've never seen her
fluff a show.*

—Minnie Pearl

When Tanya Tucker began to make her first noise on
the country concert tour scene ABC television was in
the middle of a four-year run with a show about a family
who hit the road and made sweet music. "The Partridge
Family" was a musical sitcom that scored solid numbers
for most of its run. Two decades later it would become
somewhat of a cult classic. In a very unique way, it was
an oversimplified rock version of the Tuckers' life.

Most of the millions of viewers who tuned in to watch
Shirley Jones, David Cassidy and company ride their old
school bus around the country from gig to gig must have
thought the show's writers strayed a long way from the
truth. One look at Tanya Tucker's early road life might
have caused even the most casual viewer to reassess the
Partridge family's old bus and the bizarre things that
could happen when chasing from one date to another
with a family in tow.

Early on there was no bus for Tanya Tucker. The
Tuckers didn't have enough money to make that kind of
investment. They hit the road in the family car, stayed in
the cheapest motels, washed clothes in Laundromats or
their room's sink, ate at burger joints, and traveled all
night long. It was a tough grind filled with life-and-death

risks. Close calls were almost as common as bugs on the windshield.

Cars and country music had long been tragically linked. Countless stars like Patsy Cline had been all but killed in car crashes on late night dark roads. Johnny Horton, a man with huge potential, had been lost in that fashion. Long hours, little sleep, and one-night stands hundreds of miles apart would seem to make this more the business of the grim reaper than the modern day pied piper. Yet, this is the way of the business.

On May 7, 1973, even before she had a chance to really begin her career, Tanya Tucker's shot at the big time almost ended on an open stretch of rural Texas highway. Near Brady, Texas, as the Tuckers raced to get to a Uvalde, Texas, date, the driver somehow lost control of the car. The crash sent four people to the hospital. Beau broke both his arms and had to have them set in casts. Juanita was even more severely injured. She was laid up with a broken back. Fortunately she suffered no permanent damage. Tanya somehow escaped with only facial scratches and a few bruises. A day later she was able to perform. Yet that was the reality and danger of traveling long miles over back roads by car.

Eventually, this brush with death, combined with a few royalty checks would lead to Beau tracking down a good used tour bus. But that was still a few months away. As it was, he had to learn to drive with casts on his arms and pray that he would stay awake on the long, dark nights.

Columbia, convinced that their little girl was the real deal, was now investing heavily in promoting Tanya. Any kind of accident which would knock her out of working would be a heavy blow to the company. The company breathed a huge sigh of relief when the next night Tanya was back at work with the recording giant's other young artist, Johnny Rodriguez. They didn't have enough music in the can to wait out a long hospital stay. Business required that they strike iron with a healthy little girl now, or not at all.

The Tucker/Rodriguez teaming which the label dreamed up seemed to be a natural. Both were young, Tanya now coming up on fifteen and Johnny just past twenty. Both had initial releases that made the top ten. Johnny had even started this year, 1973, with the #1 "You Always Come Back to Hurting Me." Most importantly, both were drawing kids to concert venues. In an arm of the music business that had long been dominated by older Americans, a youth movement was something which Columbia couldn't afford to turn its back on. What a concept—kids, with their large amounts of disposable money, loving country music. Who could blame the label for trying to cash in on the market which had driven rock 'n' roll cash registers for almost two decades? This was a marketing gimmick that might even spin a whole new market for their product. If successful it could change the way Nashville did business.

Mostly using house bands, Tanya and Johnny worked almost anywhere with a microphone and lights. They traveled from Florida to Illinois, from Texas to Maine. Occasionally Tanya even made it back home to Henderson. It was a breakneck pace, but it had its rewards. There were hundreds of interviews, scores of trips to radio stations, and lots of cameras and media focused on this new young breed of country star. Each night when Tucker/Rodriguez closed their set with a duet of the old country standard "Burning Bridges," it all but brought the house down. It seemed that in America's small towns country's youngest guns were firing live ammunition and hitting the bull's-eye almost every time.

At this point Tanya was almost everyone's teenage country sweetheart. Established artists loved to have a picture taken with her, fans asked her to sign everything, and teenage boys chased after her as if she were a teen sex symbol, and in a way she was. Still sweet and demurely dressed on stage, there was a twinkle in her eyes and a growl in her voice that seemed to set off most boys and some men. These reactions were much too strong to be a crush, but Tanya was too young for Nashville's press to call it anything else without being unseemly. So rather than confront the fact that Tanya was starting to hit the audience in more places than the heart, they chose to ignore it. Back home in Nashville, a producer was making note of Tanya's sexual presence.

Billy Sherrill knew that he and the label had to have a follow-up to "Dawn" and "Jamestown." They needed a song that would climb the charts and keep Tanya on top. Working with a child in such an adult world meant that there could be no false steps or mistakes. He had to guess right. Using his years of experience as his guide, Sherrill opted for another story song.

At first Billy Sherrill wasn't even sure he wanted to cut "What's Your Mama's Name." When he initially listened to the Dallas Frazier/Earl Montgomery penned tune, he thought it too bland for Tanya.

"I thought it was a mediocre song," he remembered, "until the very last line. In fact I wasn't even going to cut it until I heard 'and her eyes are Wilson green.'"

That line sold it to Billy. He then sold it to Tanya, and the latter had no problem selling it to the world. Ironically she wasn't the first person to cut it. George Jones had recorded it with Sherrill earlier, but the great one didn't push it as a single. For the legendary Jones it remained an album cut. So it was still a virgin in the single sense of the word.

Tanya's version of "What's Your Mama's Name" hit the chart on March 24, 1973, and climbed steadily. It would hang tough for almost two months before peaking at #1 on May 19, 1973. It knocked Roy Clark of "Hee Haw" off the top spot. "Come Live With Me" would be Clark's only #1 cut, but Tanya wouldn't have to worry about it being her only #1 for long. The total chart time of seventeen weeks for "Name" equaled "Delta Dawn." This release would become Tanya's all-time greatest as far as chart success, yet it was only the beginning of her chart toppers. With this song's climb Sherrill was sure that his newest artist would last for a long time.

As Tanya rode to the top of the charts again, she stopped her national tour long enough to remember someone who had given her a break in the past. Judy Lynn called and offered to help get Columbia's new little star on a Nevada stage. Responding to that call Tanya soon found herself sharing the spotlight not only with Lynn, but with the Mills Brothers show at the Flamingo Hotel.

Before Judy introduced Tanya, she reminded the audience that she was the one who discovered this child-wonder. Then she would go on to tell the largely country music ignorant crowd about all of "this sweet little girl's" successes.

The crowd was therefore prepared for something of a cross between Shirley Temple and one of television's Brady girls. In the back of their minds they were ready to give the kid a break and like her even if she was young and unpolished. They were determined to be polite, they certainly weren't prepared to be blown away.

Maybe it was because she was in the city that Elvis ruled. Maybe it was the fact that she had recently seen the King work and gotten a feel for how he put the audience under a spell. Maybe it was just that she had gained so much in a few months on the road that she was ready to explode. Whatever it was, the "sweet little girl" in the very modest dress took no prisoners. Working with a competent band, she sang with power and moved like a cat. She didn't grab the crowd, she pounced on them. She growled and purred, and they followed her every motion, hung on her every word. Brenda Lee may have been "Little Miss Dynamite," but

Tanya had become something even more powerful. She was "The Texas Tornado."

Her energy and drive left the audience breathless. When she sang of pain, they felt it. When she warbled about desire, they all got hot. When she wiggled, they sighed. When she waved good-bye, they cried out for more. In the past she had been entertaining and good, but now she was a professional who could be put on stage with any country act and hold her own. She was ready for the top and craving bigger audiences. She was the kind of opener who made closers cuss!

The reviewers noted this too. One wrote, "She is graceful, confident, and handled the mike like a pro. Even in front of an audience used to the very best, she was completely in control. She looks more like Shirley Temple than a soon-to-be sex symbol . . . yet in her eyes and grin the fire is evident."

With the reviews in mind and Tanya's show-stopping poise burned into his memory, Beau vowed not to bring her back to Vegas until someone offered her top spot in one of the big rooms. In just a few months this fire would break out with a flame that would have everyone talking about the teenage tigress.

Tanya needed a strong follow-up single to "What's Your Mama's Name." Sherrill and Columbia opted for a tune penned by master song scribe Curly Putman. The title referred to the Georgia sunset, but from the second it hit the charts it was obvious that "Blood Red and Goin' Down" was headed anywhere but downward.

"I just loved it," Tanya still says of the cut. "I knew that it was for me from the start."

"Blood Red and Goin' Down" (released July 1973) ended with a double murder, but for the recording artist it was anything but the end of the line. For a week in September she held #1 again. This time she knocked out the legendary "Crown Prince of Country Music," Conway Twitty. Twitty had firmly held onto the top spot for three weeks with "You've Never Been This Far Before." In Tanya's case, she had been to the top before, and she would jump on for the return trip several more times. "Blood Red" stayed in the Billboard rankings until it was time to carve the Thanksgiving turkey.

Tanya was now an occasional guest at the "Mother Church" of country music. On the Opry stage she not only thrilled the audience, but the old-timer performers. Stars like Connie Smith and Roy Acuff had their pictures taken with her. Kitty Wells bragged about her. Minnie Pearl took her under her wing. She was welcomed like few others had been—she was welcomed as both a child and a star.

Offstage the "little girl with the big voice" was beginning to really work the press. She had figured out that the best way to get ink was to make statements that seemed a bit too brash and cocky for a new star who had yet to get a driver's license.

"I plan to retire by twenty-six," she told reporters. "I will be married by twenty-eight, have a couple of kids and kick back."

She may have been talking about kicking back, but on stage she was slowly turning up the heat. She somehow sensed that bumping and grinding a bit not only worked the audience up, but created controversy. Controversy in turn kept her name in the press and people at her show. With that in mind, her next song choice was perfect.

With two straight #1s under her belt, it was time for Sherrill and Tucker to again pull out some magic. They wanted a single that would continue to make people notice the now fifteen-year-old girl. They also had both theorized that Tanya's ability to titillate in concert just might be something that worked just as well in the recording studio. To find the right controversial single they turned to one of country music's best known outlaws, David Allan Coe.

Unlike many others who had adopted the title, Coe himself had earned the outlaw label. An ex-convict, he was a big, surly-looking fellow. He scared folks. People would walk across the street to avoid meeting him face-to-face. Folks who knew him well, and those were very few, were amazed that a body could contain that many tattoos. Early in his career he had recorded songs that would have earned X-ratings in theaters. Worse than that, he was supposed to be as despicable as he was mean-looking. No one really knew what to do with him.

Many producers who recognized his genius for writing, still couldn't find enough courage to even call him and arrange a meeting. Others didn't want to deal with him because they feared what would happen to them if they turned him down.

Yet this hombre with the reputation for fights had a few soft spots. Caught up in the power of love that he had witnessed firsthand in his brother's life, he wrote a very gentle and passionate poem entitled "Tell Me Lady, Can You Pray." He gave it to his brother as a wedding present. After adding music to the poem, Coe realized that he might have a hit. He was convinced that this time he had caught lightning in a bottle. Yet one look in the mirror told him that this song was probably meant for someone other than himself.

Confident of an easy sale, he took the song to Columbia. When Coe played it for Sherrill, the producer didn't understand what the song meant. "What do you mean, lay with me in a field of stone?" Most people, including at first Sherrill, assumed that *lay* referred to having sex in a field.

Coe then explained that it represented the two lovers not only living together for all their life, but being buried side by side and resting together forever. It was a wonderful, beautiful sentiment, one that must have surprised Sherrill. After all Coe didn't seem like the love poem type.

Sherrill thought about the controversy of that signature line for a while and then talked Coe into changing the title to "Would You Lay With Me (in a Field of Stone)." Sherrill also assured Coe that he could find a place for the tune with one of his artists.

If it had taken the producer a while to understand the song's meaning, it would take Beau Tucker even longer. In spite of the fact that Sherrill assured the Tuckers that this was the perfect follow-up for the teenage hit maker, Beau didn't like it. It was too adult, too illicit for his innocent daughter. Tanya, perhaps reacting to her father, wasn't caught up in the song either. She thought that it wasn't catchy enough and to her it didn't seem to have much commercial appeal. Yet Sherrill wouldn't give up. He was now completely hooked on the song and insisted that it was the perfect tune for Tanya. So he persisted.

With several reservations, Tanya finally walked into the recording studio and began to work with the musicians and Billy. It wasn't until the end, when in final production Sherrill added a haunting roundlike conclusion to "Would You Lay With Me," that almost everyone felt that it was right. Beau still didn't like what it could mean to his daughter's image. He didn't want it released and he didn't want her singing it on stage.

Over Beau's objections the song was released two weeks into 1974, and from day one it created controversy. In many circles it seemed that father was right. Several of the reporting stations would not play it. They deemed its message and implications too adult for a little fifteen-year-old girl to be singing. These same stations probably wouldn't have balked if it had been Dolly Parton or Barbara Mandrell who had released it, but this was a "little girl," and in their minds it just wasn't morally responsible to condone a record label using her in this fashion.

"She shouldn't be singing about going to bed with anyone!" some critics harshly stated.

Some went further.

"She shouldn't even be thinking about it!"

As would come to be the case so often in the singer's career, "Would You Lay With Me" created a golden opportunity for Tanya to get her name in front of the press because of controversy. The little dynamo grabbed the chance with gusto and pushed her innocence to the limit. She wondered why anyone was concerned about the song's message. They didn't listen. They didn't understand. The message was really sweet, not illicit. She only hoped that someday some man would love her that much. In concerts and in the press she continued to plead the song's case. She answered every protest with one of her own. She quickly hit back every negative volley with a positive return.

Without really knowing it, the media was creating a monster. Tanya watched as the negative press kept her in the public eye like she had never been before. She was beginning to understand the old Hollywood rule, "The only thing worse than being talked about is not being talked about." With a sly smile on her face she listened to people phone stations to request the tune so they could hear what all the fuss was about. Those calls generated sales and other requests. The song thus became hotter than she or Sherrill could have ever imagined. Even magazines like *Playboy* and *Rolling Stone* were taking note of it.

On March 30, with some people still boiling over the words and message, Tanya had another #1 song. Ironically she again knocked Conway Twitty out of the top spot. This time Twitty was reminding listeners that "There's a Honky Tonk Angel Who'll Take Me Back In." With "Lay With Me" Tanya would begin to build a reputation that would put her in the same league as Conway's honky-tonk angel.

With the great success spurned on by her records and show-stopping performances, Tanya was in demand on the road and for guest shots on Nashville-based syndicated television shows. It was therefore time for a move. The Tuckers left Nevada behind and journeyed to a farm outside of Nashville in Ashland City, Tennessee. With horses, dogs, cats and a wide variety of other animals, it was not only Tanya's refuge but it appeared to be an animal refuge as well. The estate had 220 acres. It would seem an ideal place for a child to spend time, a modern Sunnybrook Farm. With rolling pastures, bulls gently grazing, the sight of the Cumberland River rolling along the edge of the property, old oak and fruit trees, what little princess could ask for anything more? Yet the demands of doing more than two hundred shows a year would make this new "perfect" home more a place to store things than live. With that in mind it came time to invest in a piece of equipment that would really serve as the family's home.

After shopping around town, Beau found just what he needed. It didn't have a swimming pool and four bedrooms, but it did have tires, a diesel engine and bunks. Beau was more than proud to write the check for Sonny James's old touring bus. One of the few changes he made was to have Tanya Tucker painted on the side.

Sonny James, the Southern Gentleman, had been performing and churning out hits since the early fifties. Because he was a huge Music City star and a great talent, his old bus had seen a lot of miles. It happened that at just about the same time that Beau and Tanya were hungry for the road, Sonny was getting tired of the one-night stands. Just a few years before he had recorded more #1 hits in a row than Columbia's hot new teen star had recorded birthdays. Now he was getting a bit older and wanted to slow down. The hits didn't mean as much to him as they used to. He was more than happy to watch his bus disappear down the road without his being on it. He was only too eager to leave the rugged grind of the road for the solitude of country living away from the spotlight.

The bus would mean a big change for Tanya and her family. Most of that change was good. One facet of it was a bit sad.

Tanya was still a young girl. She owned a huge Saint Bernard named Wendell, a mutt named Pumpkin and a horse that could ride like the wind. She thought of herself as a "4-H kind of kid," but cared nothing about cooking or sewing. She was a tomboy with a gentle heart, as well as a tough kid who intimidated adults and charmed children. She was country music's Fonz before he ever appeared on the air. She was cool in an industry that in the past hadn't paid much attention to being cool. And parents, as well as kids, flocked to her everywhere she went. Yet, she wasn't normal, not anymore.

She no longer had time to ride bikes or play in the grass. She was far too busy to talk on the phone about nothing and flirt with neighborhood boys. She was much too famous to even be left alone for a few seconds. More and more fame was removing her from people her own age and the normal situations and experiences that went with being a teenager. Finally, as Tanya began her first big bus tour across the country, she gave up the last facet of normal life she had clung to. She dropped out of school in the ninth grade.

"I was bored," she told the press and friends. "I was in a class that was geared to choosing a career. I already knew what I wanted to do. I was doing it. School wasn't going to get me anywhere I wasn't going to go without it."

In a very real sense she was right. She had quickly outgrown school and classes. She didn't have a need for the standard educational training. Still it seemed a shame that she never had a chance to be homecoming queen or a cheerleader. Yet how many of her classmates got to appear on the cover of national magazines and meet Elvis backstage? All things considered, Tanya probably got the best end of the trade-off. Still, one has to wonder.

In her bio she stated, "My heart is in music." Another publicity release described Tanya as "one whale of a talent. To know her is to know that she is a sweetheart, with a quick sense of humor and a deep, intense mind and a fierce determination to fulfill her goals. Tanya Tucker will be a STAR!"

Now she was going to have a chance to prove that her heart was in music and that she really was willing to pay stardom's huge price. Life on the road, even for a pubescent sex object who was reminding more and more people of a female Elvis, would not be easy. If the Tuckers were going to hang in for the long haul or be blown out by the pressures would be determined by the long coast to coast, border to border ribbon of concrete they were now heading down at a mile a minute.

Chapter Six

The Country Road

I want to be labeled like an Elvis. I would love to be bunched with the best. After all, who is any higher than Elvis?

—*Tanya Tucker*

Anyone who has ever believed the life of a country music star is one filled with glamour has never been on the road for a long haul of one-night stands. For Tanya Tucker and her family the long, seemingly never ending grind was just beginning. In an old bus with a new group of guys simply known as the band, and with a notebook full of bookings that stretched across the country, this introduction to an entertainer's real life-style was going to be a tough one. What a challenge it is for the new-comer. As was often the case, shows sometimes were as far as six hundred miles from one another. Just getting to the next venue in time to set up and get on stage was a herculean challenge.

Things were always made easier when a large group of fans arrived early just to watch the bus pull in and park or when others would motor up beside the bus as it cruised down the road and wave and honk their horns. That, and sold tickets, were the assurance that all the hard work was paying off. Still it was so tough, especially when it was almost all being accomplished by a family of newcomers.

Brother Don was at the wheel of the rig, and all the other family members were intermingled with the band. In the middle of it all, often pacing the aisles or fidgeting in her seat while she watched the countryside roll by, was Tanya. Living in a confined area with a large group of people is a life that would be hard on most teenagers. There is so little action, so few places to run off energy. No place to really be alone. Yet for the fifteen-year-old sensation, this was the way it had to be. In both private and public she was always in view, always being observed. She was in a fishbowl consisting of a bus and a stage.

During these days she would pass the time by speaking and daydreaming of a cowboy named Mike and talk of riding horses. She would subsist on a diet of mainly junk food and soda pop. She would tell visiting writers that she didn't miss not having a childhood because she really didn't know what one was. Yet she would talk about days off and doing nothing the same way most kids talked about school holidays. She was performing country sets and at the same time she was listening to Elton John, Allman Brothers, Redbone, Dave Loggins, John Denver, Gordon Lightfoot and Lobo. And that was the same kind of music that a million other girls her age were tuning in in their bedrooms. And Tanya was also studying—not math or social studies, but Elvis.

"I love his new stuff," she would tell people. It was the Vegas Elvis, the one who wore the jumpsuits and playfully drove middle-age crowds into a wild frenzy who Tanya idolized. He was probably responsible for her new look on stage and he was definitely responsible for her more "dramatic" stage movements on up-tempo songs. In so many ways, he was her hero. She dreamed of having that kind of power and adulation. She certainly talked about it at almost every stop.

At the beginning of her concert parade through the U.S., she was called "The Texas Tornado." It seemed a perfect title for country's teen sensation. Like the huge twister that tore apart Waco, Texas, a few years before Tanya was born, her force and power were wrapped in an innocent looking package. Yet even though she looked almost weak, she packed a punch and had a far-reaching voice. She had destructive force—the kind that left an audience weak-kneed and crying out for more. Yet she was evolving into something else, something more!

The five-piece band that had no name other than "Tanya's Band," was tight and solid. They knew who the star was and didn't try to upstage her. Dressed as well as any country music group on the road, they looked like they should have been on a Vegas stage and certainly this was in the back of Beau's and Tanya's minds. For them it was like every show was an audition for one of the "big" rooms on the strip.

Tanya was proud of being known as "The Texas Tornado." She fully appreciated just what that handle meant. Yet as the months rolled by and the reviewers wrote more and more about Tanya's performances, another analogy came up time and time again, and Tanya seemed to cling to it even more than she had the "early storm warning."

"When she comes on stage it is like she is the female Elvis," wrote a half-dozen folks at different times during the tour. And why did they think she was so much like Elvis? Obviously her racy movements and an occasional sneer had something to do with it. The driving old rock 'n' roll rhythms that were used on several of her numbers also brought out an attitude that seemed to have some of the Presley swagger. But more than anything else it was the way the crowds, especially the young teen and preteen boys and their fathers, reacted to her. It was more lust than love. She was like no woman who had ever come into country music, and she still wasn't of age to be the woman she was!

"I want to be labeled like an Elvis," she would tell dozens of reporters. "I would love to be bunched with the best. After all, who is any higher than Elvis?" Who indeed?

Like "the King," Tanya drew a huge amount of attention—some of it far from positive. Not even old enough to drive, Tanya was constantly hit on by disc jockeys, promoters and fans. She was being treated like a woman —a full-blooded, full-grown sex goddess, but she was still in so many ways a little girl.

Sensing the serious problems that could arise because of this mixed perception, Beau made sure that his daughter was never alone. She couldn't tour a fair's midway alone. Don even accompanied her to the ladies' room. She was like the teen idols of another era, except she was drawing attention from people who hadn't been teenagers in decades. It was a little bit scary for her father.

Tanya had given up the little girl dresses and now wore leather and showed a bit more skin during her shows. When the impassioned men got just a glimpse of her belly button, they let out wild howls of approval. In a bizarre, almost perverted sense, she was a sex symbol not unlike Harlow or Monroe, at the same time she was sporting training bras.

Tanya was opening for stars like Loretta Lynn and Willie Nelson, but she wouldn't be opening for long. No one wanted to follow her. When Tanya left the stage, the audience was too drained, too washed out to respond much for the next act. Halfway through the tour she had become so hot, her show so talked about, that the bible of rock, *Rolling Stone,* sent out one of their best writers to hop on her bus and see what all the fuss was about.

Chet Flippo's cover story was entitled, "Tanya the Teenage Teaser." The article was so strong and Tanya's star seemed to be rising so fast, that she knocked all of the era's hot rock acts off page one. During the week of September 26, 1974, when folks went by a newsstand, it was a sultry teenage girl who was staring back from the cover of *Rolling Stone*. The header beside the photograph read, "Hi, I'm Tanya Tucker, I'm 15, you're gonna hear from me." This was a long way from being a "centerfold" in some of the Nashville-based country press. She was really being recognized now.

It didn't take Flippo long to figure out that the girl was something special. He wrote: "She consciously defies labels. MCs throughout the country pronounce her 'delightful.' Nashville's country stars pronounce her 'delightful.' Middle-age audiences describe her as a charming entertainer. Lechers see her as a torrid teenage sexpot and prepubescent boys look on her as a Holy Grail."

As would happen so often in her career, Tanya was open and fresh when Flippo interviewed her. She spoke for the first time about possibly going more pop. She talked about promoters already wanting to team her with Mick Jagger. She spoke of how much she loved rock crowds because they really let their emotions show. As with many interviews during this period, she already seemed bored with the country music business. She spoke of retirement in the same breath she talked about her latest single. She talked about wanting to do nothing for a while, and yet that is what she did for hours each day as the bus rolled down the road to the next gig. For the first time, this all came out in the press. The public was beginning to know what made Tanya tick.

At Milwaukee's Summerfest the little girl was ironically booked at the Schlitz Beer pavilion. Too young to drink the product, she was nevertheless old enough to sell it. Over three thousand fans turned out to listen and watch the dynamo. Next door Helen Reddy drew fifteen thousand. A few hours before Tanya took the stage she heard Reddy's version of "Delta Dawn" filtering across the fairgrounds. Shaking her head, a bit of fire in her eye, she told all those around her, "I'd like to be on that stage with Helen Reddy. I'd blow her right off that stage." In all honesty she would have probably blown her out of the state. That is how seasoned she had already become.

It may have been at that moment that Tanya began to realize that while she was already a star in country music and soon to be an even bigger one, that didn't necessarily make her a huge star in other forms of entertainment. "Dawn" was her signature song, but a "Helen-Come-Lately" was pulling in a lot more money singing it on the other side of the stream. Not yet motivated by money, Tanya wanted a piece of that "star" action so that she could prove to the world and herself she was a performer who deserved to be compared to Elvis. As much fame as she was earning, she was hungry for even more. Those around her were probably surprised by this, but Beau wasn't. He could see her drive. His job was to keep that drive focused.

So, when Tanya occasionally received a reprieve from the one-night stands, she didn't get to spend much time at home. Columbia and Billy Sherrill jerked her into the recording studio, and inside those soundproofed walls kept her going strong.

Sherrill knew a good thing when he heard it. He sensed that his success with the young singer was due to the type of song he had chosen for her. In these sessions he was sticking with the story-telling theme that had pushed her to the top. At this time, the two songs that he pulled out for singles were destined for a lot of chart time.

"The Man That Turned my Mama On" and "I Believe the South Is Gonna Rise Again" were perfect follow-ups for the country charts. The former hit #4 and the latter peaked after just breaking into the top twenty, but they weren't as strong as "Would You Lay With Me (in a Field of Stone)". Around Nashville, where stars sometimes faded as quickly as they appeared, people began wondering if Columbia's teenage star's luster and magic had begun to dim. Had she peaked? Was her sexy, almost raw, concert image beginning to hurt her at the stores? Were true country fans uncomfortable with a teenager who acted a bit like a Lolita?

One of those who seemed to buy into the "fading star" theory was Columbia. They had made a lot of money from Tanya, but they seemed to sense that the well was too dry to invest much more capital. When her contract ran out, they let MCA outbid them for her services. This meant the end of Tanya's work with Billy Sherrill and the beginning of a movement that would see her expand into a new area of the business. It was a huge turning point in her young life.

Putting a million dollars up front showed that MCA had a great deal of faith and a lot of plans for Tanya. Rather than buying the diminishing audience concept, they actually believed that there was a huge new base of customers waiting to spend money on the product if the label could just get them to listen to this hot new act. In their minds Tanya might not have been the female Elvis, but she just might be a white Diana Ross. With that in mind they set about finding the perfect person to welcome Tanya to MCA's family.

Los Angeles producer Snuff Garrett was chosen to guide Tanya in her first session in MCA's West Coast studio. He was used to working with pop artists. He had even been responsible for comedian Vicki Lawrence's monster crossover hit "The Night the Lights Went Out in Georgia." That song was very much like the ones which had become Tanya's signature pieces. One of Garrett's other clients, Cher, also was scoring on the rock charts with story tunes. MCA wanted him to find one that would create that kind of stir for their "Million Dollar Teenager."

This thought pattern would have seemed very logical. "What's Your Mama's Name" had hit the bottom of the rock chart, and "Blood Red and Going Down," "Delta Dawn," "The Man That Turned my Mama On" and "Would You Lay With Me (in a Field of Stone)" had all showed movement on the bigger and more listened to radio stations. The last tune had crept as high as #46 on the rock charts. Armed with these statistics, MCA figured that Columbia had definitely missed the boat by not going L.A. with Tanya and pushing her like Glen Campbell as a crossover artist.

The song that was marked for MCA's first Tucker release had been written by Kenny O'Dell and Larry Henley and seemed to be inspired by the Burt Lancaster movie *The Rainmaker.* A few names were changed, but other than that, "Lizzie and the Rainman" read a great deal like the two-hour motion picture script. Strangely enough, this first choice was anything but a brand-new song. "Lizzie" had been recorded several times before Snuff picked it up. Many in his office thought it would end on a Cher album he was producing. It seemed perfect for the rock queen. Instead he tried it on his newcomer. In a very real sense it worked. Tanya's voice caressed and worked it as if it had been written with Tanya Tucker in mind.

Released in May of 1975, "Lizzie" quickly shot up the country charts peaking at the top position on June 13. It was Tanya's fourth country #1! It also made some noise on the rock side of the ledger. The week before it peaked in Nashville, it cracked Billboard's Rock Top Forty. It would hang on at #37 for two weeks then quickly fade away. While it was a nice showing, MCA had hoped for more. In all honesty, so had the star.

Tanya and Beau didn't seem to feel right working with Snuff. They weren't ready to make the L.A. move yet. At this point they both preferred the laid-back atmosphere of Nashville much better. They discussed this between them and suggested to MCA's West Coast office that better music and production could be found in

Music City. MCA wasn't as sure as the Tuckers, but they had invested enough in this star that they wanted to make sure they recouped their investment. So they bowed to Tanya and Beau's desires. After only one album MCA let their sixteen-year-old star temporarily go home to record. Still her L.A. work with Snuff would reap some rewards and give the label a reason to want to eventually bring Tanya back west.

Tanya's next release from her West Coast sessions, "San Antonio Stroll," was a straight country song with no designs on the pop market. Peter Noah, who had never been to the title city, wrote the number. Garrett had contacted the struggling songwriter in Hawaii and asked if he had any material that would be right for Tanya Tucker. Noah sent the producer "Stroll." It would turn out to be Noah's only real hit in the music business (he did earn both money and fame as a television writer/producer), and for Tanya it would simply be another #1, the fifth for the teenage country superstar. The song hit the pinnacle just two weeks after Tanya's seventeenth birthday.

This period was a unique one in Tanya's recording career. Not only was MCA plugging her work and pushing through a big publicity effort to get her songs to the top, but Columbia was also releasing some of the older cuts that they had in their vaults. In a very real sense Tanya was flooding the market. To the listening audience it must have seemed that she was releasing a new cut every few months. And in reality, that is the way it was!

While MCA was scoring big with "Lizzie" and "Stroll," Columbia was seeing moderate success with "Spring" and "Greener Than the Grass," two cuts that had originally been deemed unfit as singles. With their rival's success, coupled with their own sales of once thought of "second-rate" material, Columbia must have been second-guessing themselves for not resigning

Tanya. Anyone could see that she wasn't fading and that the skies seemed to be the limit for the superstar.

Still, even with the top charting songs, compared to rock, country music didn't score big with albums. The truth was, sales of fifty thousand units were usually considered pretty good. A hit album might average no more than twice that. Columbia had released three albums during Tanya's three years with them. "Delta Dawn," "What's Your Mama's Name" and "Would You Lay With Me," had all done well in a country sense—selling at least one hundred thousand copies. Yet it was only after they had lost their prized product that the label may have sensed just what a golden goose they had called their own. "Tanya Tucker's Greatest Hits" moved rapidly for the now lame-duck label. As the numbers rolled in, Columbia must have looked over at the MCA offices and kicked themselves. They had literally put a cash cow out to pasture far too soon. As if to emphasize that point, "Greatest Hits" went gold. It must have hurt the label a great deal to send Tanya the award that went along with this lofty sales plateau.

MCA looked at the numbers for "Greatest Hits" and rubbed their hands with glee. They surely realized that a lot of the folks who were buying the album didn't fit the normal demographic mold for country music consumers. These buyers were younger and just as prone to listen to rock or pop. In a very real sense, this gold record seemed to prove their original assessment of Tanya's star potential beyond country music.

In a stroke of either imaginative genius or as a tribute to her growing popularity and fame, MCA's first album release on their new star was simply called "Tanya Tucker." At initial inspection it embraced the story-telling theme that had made the teen a hot hit producer at Columbia. Yet underneath Garrett had done a bit of fine-tuning. Songs like "Son-of-a-Preacherman," "Love of a Rolling Song" and "Someday Soon" were more pop/rock oriented. Their roots weren't Music City. Watching and gauging reaction to these subtle moves would help MCA begin to formulate a plan to introduce Tanya to a larger audience. They had their eyes on the future. Meanwhile, they needed a new producer and a batch of country hits right now.

With a move back to a Music City venue in 1976, MCA had to search for a producer who could replace Garrett and still work some magic with their act. Out of that search came an association that would last even until this moment.

Tanya Tucker and Jerry Crutchfield got together for the first time through the direction of MCA. Jerry was a veteran producer who had a great reputation throughout the industry. Unlike Billy Sherrill, Crutchfield had never tied himself to one label. Like Tanya, he was independent and thrived on doing his own thing in his own way. He didn't want limits placed on him. He didn't want CEOs looking over his shoulder. He felt his successes spoke loud enough that he didn't need monitoring.

Over the course of several years Jerry had brought hits to people as diverse as Barbara Fairchild and Dave Loggins. He may have lived in Music City, but he understood music everywhere. It didn't take long for MCA and Beau Tucker to realize that he was the perfect man at the perfect time for Tanya. Tanya instantly felt comfortable in Crutchfield's hands and the "Lovin' & Learnin' " album proved that they could produce as well as the Tucker/Sherrill team had. Their first session generated some impressive songs including "Don't Believe my Heart Can Stand Another You," which peaked at the fourth spot, "You've Got Me to Hold Onto," which topped out at #3, and Tanya's sixth chart-topper "Here's Some Love." To all appearances she would continue her domination of the country charts for many years ahead. After all, she was just now beginning to reach maturity. Yet there was something new brewing just beneath the surface.

On October 9, 1976, just one day before Tanya's eighteenth birthday, Conway Twitty knocked "The Texas Tornado" out of #1 with "The Games That Daddies Play." It would be a long time before she reached the top point again. For Tanya her days in country music were all but over. She and MCA had bigger plans— much bigger plans. Yet before she left the country for the city, she did produce a few more magic moments.

The first of those, "Ridin' Rainbows," released in December 1976, almost made it to the top ten. It peaked at #12. "It's a Cowboy Lovin' Night," issued in March of 1977 hit #7, and "You Are So Beautiful" pushed onto the market in July as Columbia's last release of old stock. It came in at #40. On the album side "Here's Some Love," "Ridin' Rainbows" and "You Are So Beautiful" scored in the same fashion as Tanya's other long-playing releases. MCA's version of "Tanya Tucker's Greatest Hits" did even better. Yet times were changing and Tanya wanted more. She now knew where she wanted to be, it was just a matter of finding the right people to take her there. While she and Beau had wanted to make the move back to Nashville the previous year, now that she had come of age, L.A. looked appealing again.

The county fairs, the smaller and more reserved country crowds, the silly appearances on television specials like "Circus of American Music," filmed in Nashville with Dennis Weaver, Sandy Duncan, Jim Stafford and Jonelle Allen, were beginning to hold her back from a shot at worldwide stardom. On the bus she was tired of the lack of privacy and the all-night poker games. She wanted a more active social life. She was a big fish in a small pond. Country wasn't expanding fast enough to make her a strong power in all facets of the entertainment industry. She was weary of an existence

where LaCosta and Don sold photos and tapes before
and after the shows. She was also ready for her father to
stop working around the clock just to keep her on top.
She wanted more for everyone.

Tanya told writer Richard Nusser, "I don't need dope
and things like that to make me happy 'cause I've got
other things on my mind that'll make me a lot happier
. . . I think being yourself, being satisfied with yourself.
My parents have brought me up to be different, not to
follow along with everybody but to be the leader." Tanya
was ready to lead her own life. She was ready to step out
on her own and take control. She was ready for some
bold new steps.

In her bio she stated, "I still have a lot to do. I'd like
to be as professional as I can, to be able to go on stage
with the biggest stars, with the best."

At this point, outside of the south and rural areas in
the north and west, country music was still looked upon
as a second-rate product. Rarely did even the hottest
performers like Tanya get to show off their wares in the
largest, newest, nicest auditoriums. More often than not
they were working with mediocre lighting and bad
sound systems in older coliseums and indoor rodeo facilities. It could be a grind, especially if you had ambi-
tion, and Tanya had lots of that.

Tanya wanted to grow and expand. She was young and
at the beginning of her career. She had a desire to play
the same places Elvis worked. She wanted to own the
big rooms in Vegas and a chance to headline her own
network special. She wanted to move up a notch and see
if she could duke it out at the next level.

"I don't want to be around mediocre people," she
told friends and writers. With this statement and a great
deal of thought, she worked with MCA to put together a
new product—one that would make everyone sit up and
notice Tanya Tucker! She was ready to say good-bye to
that long ribbon of concrete known as the country road.

- Chapter Seven -

The Move to a New Kind of Music

Tanya Tucker is very special. She sings with as many textures in her voice as there are colors in a rainbow.

—**Melody Maker** *(a London-based music magazine)*

*S*ometime in the months just before 1976 MCA and Tanya seriously began to think of going after a wider audience. The record label's reason was obvious—profit. They had risked a million-dollar contract on the young woman, and they were planning on having it pay off big. In the collective mind of the Los Angeles office, country was not going to bring them a large enough harvest. They wanted more. They sensed that to maximize their opportunities they were going to have to try something radical.

Tanya's reasons for wanting to escape the country charts and concert tours were much more personal than her label's reasons. She had long been motivated by challenges. Once she had been motivated to enter a talent show or talk her way on stage with a major star for a guest shot. Then she became focused on pushing to become a top country act, to close shows and push her songs to the top of the charts. Now, she was not challenged by what she saw in Nashville. The country music audience was just too small a segment of the American society. She wanted more. She was going to have to work to get new audiences that were listening to a different type of music. It just happened to be the same kind of music she was listening to. It seemed a perfect marriage.

"Once my goal was to have a hit record," Tanya explained to those around her at that time. "Now I would say my goal is to be happy as I get older and for my family, who has worked so hard for me, to be happy too. . . . I want to be more versatile. I want to be known as a singer who sings all kinds of music."

It was the latter part of that statement that seemed to stick in peoples' minds. Tanya didn't like anything that limited her. She wanted to push envelopes, not accept their pat boundaries. More and more, country music seemed to be stifling her expression and her ability to expand her career. Feeling like a caged wild animal, she was looking for a way to escape. Of course when animals escape from the zoo, it also makes headlines and scares people. Tanya's dramatic flight would be no different. Still, for a while she marked time and waited for the right moment.

LaCosta, who had signed with and earned a few minor hits with the Capitol label, had not experienced the success in country her sister had. Nor had the talented young woman gotten a great deal of support with promotions and backing. Tanya loved her sister a great deal, and this treatment may have also helped cool the teenage star on Music City. In a way, Tanya might have figured that LaCosta would have a better shot at becoming a real country music star if little sister was in a different field.

Her other sibling's life had changed a great deal too. Don was married, had a child, and Tanya didn't want him to devote more time to her than he did to his own family. He was ready and needed to cut back. Tanya sensed that both of her siblings needed their space—a chance at their own lives—but she still felt responsible for them because they had given her so much for so long. She had to come up with a way to accomplish her goals and help them at the same time.

On the road the loneliness of being always kept out of harm's way and a normal life began to get to her in a huge and destructive way. No longer was she just bored, she was trying to do something about it. Drinking to pass time had long been a part of the country music road scene. Tanya had been introduced to it by members of her band. It goes without saying that she started to drink too soon and by this time in her career most around her thought that she was drinking way too much. She maintained her problem wasn't drinking, it was boredom. She needed more to do and more goals to reach out and go after. She was a different Tanya, and she was one who was going to be a great deal more difficult to guide.

At eighteen Tanya was no longer just another cute little girl. She was a full-blown sultry woman. So, her desires fit her body. She was simply ready for bigger things. Using a brand-new bus she was now working places like Jamboree USA in Wheeling, West Virginia, and some of the biggest fairs in the United States and Canada. Appearing in Elvis-like jumpsuits she was tearing the audiences up with her blend of country and old-fashioned rock 'n' roll.

At that time one of her most popular concert songs was Elvis's "Burning Love." Several critics as well as Asleep At The Wheel's Ray Bensen would marvel at a "flat-chested girl bumping and grinding a crowd of middle-aged men into a frenzy." Yet in the past, because she had been just a little girl, she hadn't upset or threatened the women in crowds. Now they were picking on something that the press called "That Evil Look." Many country music females didn't like the way their men responded to it. It was too raw and too passionate.

Tanya had oozed sex in an old-fashioned way up until

this point. She was like Harlow, she walked it, she talked it, but she had so much power, men questioned getting involved with her. When you watched her you forgot she was a teenager barely old enough to date. Mesmerized by movement and the sway that often caused boys to blush or worse, she was as much a woman as Raquel Welch, but she was safe. Now she was at the age to no longer be considered a pretender. When she moved she was a contender! It was okay to hit on her and talk about sex.

Some critics believed that it was this much more blatant sex appeal that would kill Tanya in country music. This was one of the envelopes she simply couldn't push. In country, females weren't up-front about sex, they were flirts. They might sing about it, even talk about it playfully, but they would never encourage men to lust after them on stage. It was too improper. It just wasn't done, until now. And if sex didn't sign her career death warrant, then another tried-and-true industry rule would.

Old beyond her years, Tanya had been to Germany, Canada and Mexico. She had an audience of young country music fans that stretched around the world. She was famous, but in the back of everyone's mind was a rarely voiced but important question. Was she going to just fade away like most child stars had when they reached their upper teens?

The question was a fair one. Brenda Lee had peaked and then faded. So had another teenage rock 'n' roller, Leslie Gore. Gore was sixteen when she set the world on fire, but by the time she was twenty no one wanted to come to her party. Fabian, Bobby Vee, Frankie Lyman and a host of others littered the "where are they now" halls of the music industry.

On television it was much the same. The kids who starred in shows like "Leave It to Beaver," "Father

Knows Best," "Lassie," "Flipper," "Fury," and a host of others had been pushed aside. Like a piece of garbage, the industry and the fans had no use for kids who weren't little and cute anymore. They didn't want them to grow up. There were exceptions like Shelley Fabares, but these were ever so rare.

Thanks at first to the motion picture industry which had tossed off the kids from *Our Gang* and even the immortal Shirley Temple, Americans had grown used to this phenomenon. Show business and its fans seemed to believe in it as strongly as if it were one of entertainment's Ten Commandments. *Child stars shall not be seen after they get out of high school!* In Nashville many were waiting and hoping that the wicked teenager would take note of this rule. There simply wasn't room for her in the Bible Belt.

Maybe this is why Tanya and MCA wanted to make the big switch. Maybe they were frightened that Tanya would become an overripe commodity in Music City. With a move to a new audience, this child star might be accepted as a young adult, not a former child star. In pop and rock there would be a fan base which would have no preconceived ideas about her because they hadn't been exposed to her. She would be brand-new. With her poise and stage presence, she should come out of the gate at full gallop and take rock by storm. It seemed almost a sure thing. But there were things to consider.

How to change her country—hayseed—image would be the major problem that faced them. She was not the innocent country girl, but it was a trap into which she seemed to fall. And it was in large part the fault of the label that now wanted her to be something else. For some time most MCA publicity pieces still described her offstage persona as "your typical teenager." Yet Tanya was a lot more than a "cute as a button, wholesome as milk, a smart, spirited cheerleader without a team." She was not a prom date without a dance. Changing her sexy on stage but never been kissed offstage image would be like trying to make Doris Day over into Marilyn Monroe. Something radical was going to have to be done to get people's attention.

As MCA played with the image problem, James Burton had been brought in to help Tanya with her road show. Burton was not the least bit country. He had been a part of the featured band which had unknowingly begun the music video business doing bits with Rick Nelson at the end of the "Ozzie and Harriet Show." He had played lead guitar for almost every famous rock performer since those early days. He was by Elvis's side when the King took his fabulous show to Vegas and across America. Burton was a legend, and he knew what it took to get a band smoking. He pushed Tanya into being even more of a rocker on stage.

In the midst of trying to figure out what direction to go, how to remake herself or to leave things alone, a tragedy that caused America and the world to stop for a moment almost crushed Tanya. On August 16, 1977, when Elvis died, she went into shock. Like most of America, she couldn't believe that the King could ever pass away. He was not mortal.

Losing Elvis was like having a family member die. Tanya didn't know what to do or where to go to find the answer to *why*. As she grieved, she remembered a man she had met during one of her appearances at the Opry. Even though she had never had any kind of relationship with him or a basis for getting in touch with him and talking in a personal manner, she tracked down Glen Campbell's phone number. Without hesitation she called the man who had played guitar for Elvis on several recording sessions. She had to talk to him about the living Elvis, the one who had been the world's best entertainer.

In his biography Glen remembered being surprised to

hear from the child star. He also remembered how upset she was when she tracked him down. They spoke several times, and while his words on Presley seemed to help Tanya put things in perspective, nothing could ease her sense of loss.

August 16, 1977: Tanya would call it the "Day the Music Died." And she added as a postscript, "I lost my whole persona of a superstar when Elvis died." In a sense it may have helped her and MCA into making a difficult decision far easier.

Perhaps it was Elvis's passing which put a more urgent passion to Tanya's search for the road to superstardom. She may have been in 1977 a *Country Music* centerfold, but that didn't thrill her like it had before. Life was too short. There had to be more.

"I want to do it all, and there's so little time," she told country beat writer Stacy Harris. "I want to just keep moving forward."

Jerry Crutchfield, her soon to be former producer, sensed that she and MCA wanted to take her to another level. "Her music was always on the cutting edge of country," he would recall. "In the late seventies there was a strong pull for her to get even more contemporary." When the call for this push came, the producer knew he wouldn't be an invited participant.

Crutchfield's releases weren't giving him much of a chance either. Tanya's records were no longer hitting the top ten. Some were barely making the charts. The pressure was on to start the cash registers ringing. She was in danger of losing her solid gold image. She was close to being labeled by some as another finished child star.

As rumors flew, Tanya continued to work the road and try to combine the rowdy country show girl with the "homecoming queen" promotional materials put out by her bookers and label. She spent a great deal of time talking to the press about her hobbies such as photography, horseback riding, water-skiing and scuba diving. She loved to brag about her latest horse named "I'm a Superstar Too."

When answering questions about the direction of her career, she would now give somewhat vague answers about wanting to appeal to all audiences and work every kind of stage. But most of the talk of her moving to a new kind of music was defused by her father. Beau simply smiled and changed the subject. When writers would tell him that he was better than ever at running Tanya's career and keeping her on line for superstardom, he would tell folks, "I don't want to be remembered as Colonel Parker, the world's best promoter. I want to be remembered as the world's best daddy." He said it with so much passion, most forgot to follow up on his plans for his daughter's career.

Still to most in the press, and especially to Tanya's loyal fans, it was obvious something was going on. The concerts, which had always been on the cutting edge, were now far less country than they had been before. And Tanya, still a master show person who exuded confidence and power on stage, seemed a bit more distant. It wasn't unusual for her shows to start late, sometimes as much as an hour later than announced. While this was common in rock, it was almost unheard of in country. Only the likes of Hank Williams, Sr., Hank Williams, Jr., and George Jones had survived making this a practice. And it had hurt them.

In Tanya's case the late arrivals seemed almost to be planned. She would tell reporters, "I was on time tonight, they were just an hour early. To be a star, you're always late. Make 'em wait!" This attitude was going against the grain of the Music City establishment. It also went against Beau's concept of what an entertainer should do. But that was the way Tanya wanted it.

In a very real sense it seemed like Tanya was attempting to force country music to shut the door on her and run her off. She seemed to want them to force her out, rather than to walk away herself. From a public relations standpoint this tactic was dangerous. It could alienate a fan base that might have to carry her for a time as she established herself to a wider demographic group. Still the teenager pushed the buttons.

At an Opry appearance she was practically booed off stage. They didn't want her to sing rock on the Opry's sacred wood. They didn't like her tight clothes and risqué moves. In a very real sense, Tanya was rebelling and by doing so she was pushing herself out of country music very quickly. Worse yet, she appeared to be jumping into unknown territory without a parachute or a map.

In the early part of the year she left her Nashville farm in the hands of her parents and moved to a beautiful home on the beachfront part of Los Angeles. Beau tried to talk to her about what she had planned. He didn't want her to cut all her strings to country music. When she ignored him, he begged her to watch out for the Los Angeles businessmen. "They'll eat you like sharks." As it turned out, in a very real sense they did.

In an announcement that shocked Nashville, Tanya canceled over $1 million in country bookings. She was tossing out the country style and she didn't want to have to go back and work it anymore. The old hits were old news. She was headed for the rock side of the circuit now. She and MCA were going to transform her into a multifaceted queen. Or at least that was the plan.

While many friends hated the move, most agreed that they thought Tanya knew what she was doing. She couldn't be a female Elvis and stay locked in country music. They knew that she had always wanted to be like the King. She was motivated by challenges and she had decided to conquer every form of expression. She wanted to own Rhythm and Blues and perform in Memphis. She wanted to rock on the streets of London. She wanted it all! This was her way of getting it. They figured that she could and would.

Tanya teamed with Steve Gold and his L.A. team and formed Far Out Management, Inc. "Exactly what we are looking for," a nineteen-year-old Tanya said describing what she and Steve had in mind for her next project.

Tanya then told writer Dolly Carlisle, "In show business, everybody has a gimmick, an image. It's the thing that identifies them. My image was this little girl with a gutsy voice singing about things little girls aren't supposed to know about. It got a big reaction coming from a kid, but I can't depend on that anymore."

This was the statement that seemed to prove she was aware that it was going to take something drastic for people to both acknowledge her adulthood and give her a chance to make it as a grown-up performer. She had felt trapped by the perception of being a child star. This had bugged her and stifled her. But if she wasn't a former child star, then who was she now?

"I'm nine different people," she informed Carlisle, "as soon as you think you know one, another pops out. I haven't found my own style yet in my music, or in myself either. But when I do, I'll know it, 'cause it'll feel right." But she added a postscript that made some in Nashville feel a little bit better.

"Even though my heart is in rock, I will never leave country." So, while she obviously wanted to move on, she was having problems deciding just how to do it and just how far to go.

During this time Beau lost a bit of his control, and he knew it. Still, with Tanya telling the press that she had turned her back on the kind of music that had made her a star, he needed to do something that would both support her and explain her to those who were confused by Tanya's attitude and actions. Like a true father he was trying to smooth things over and play down his daughter's actions.

"She's never done anything to disappoint me," he informed the Nashville media. "If Tanya wanted to go to the moon, I'd be talking to the astronauts tomorrow. Anything she wants to do, I'd make a hole for her. I think if I'd been the president, I would have resigned to help Tanya with her career."

Translation: I am behind her, but I don't know if I know what she's got planned.

What Tanya needed to make the move to rock both complete and official was not words and press statements, but an album that would define her new image and new sound. She was going to call it "TNT," because she wanted it to make a huge explosion that would wake up the whole entertainment world. It would do that.

"TNT" was produced by L.A.'s Jerry Goldstein. Goldstein was a long way from Jerry Crutchfield or Billy Sherrill. With a hard-core group of rock and rockabilly players like Jerry Hobbs, Paul Leim, Jerry Scheff, Jerry Swallow and Billy Joe Walker, Jr., Goldstein and Tanya scorched the Kendun Recorders Burbank studio. Producer Jerry Goldstein stated, "Her singing has been far too one-dimensional." He then set about trying to change that. "Not Fade Away," "Heartbreak Hotel," "Brown Eyed Handsome Man," and "If You Feel It" all pushed the envelope further than Tanya had ever before pushed it—even on stage. For a part of the session Tanya pulled in Jim Seals and Dash Crofts as backup singers. This album was hot! Yet the first song to come out of the West Coast work was anything but scorching.

Her first release during this period was called "Save Me." This haunting ballad might have applied to Tanya's own struggle to find herself during this transition period, but what it was really trying to do was alert the public to the plight of baby harp seals.

In a short video she spotlighted the plight of the Animal Protection Institute's effort to stop the wanton murder of baby harp seals. While filming her video she got a chance to swim with the dolphins at Marine World in California. She was thrilled beyond words. In a way events like this were allowing her to be the child she had rarely had a chance to be.

"I had never been in a tank before," Tanya explained about the experience at Marine World. "I got in the water with this male dolphin, and it just happened to be during breeding season. He came on like gangbusters, and I just went *whoa!* He knew I was a girl, let me tell you. There was no doubt in my mind about that. It really kind of scared me."

In a surprise move, she came back to an openly hostile Nashville to preview the film that showed the seals being slaughtered. In the background she was singing "Save Me." As she took her first political stand, Tanya also seemed to toss out an olive branch to a few locals whose feelings she had hurt.

"I will always consider Nashville home, but . . ." she began. Then after talking briefly about her new work in Los Angeles she forgot about offering olive branches and declared war on almost anyone who had ever worn a fur coat. Most of the female country music singers in Music City fit into this category. As honorary chairman for the seal effort she spoke out that day about the cruel and senseless killing of these animals. She lambasted those who made or bought the coats made out of sealskin. She argued and pleaded for people to take a stand and get involved.

With no history of activism in her background, some were shocked that Tanya would be so vocal. Others cynically wrote it off as a publicity stunt. Yet those who knew her well realized that she was simply following her heart. For years she had adopted countless dogs and cats. She loved horses and petted and named her cows. A kitten or puppy could made her laugh or bring her to tears. So she took this seal campaign very seriously.

As the weeks passed she got into verbal public spats

with Canadian Prime Minister Pierre Trudeau. She argued that his comparing the killing of baby seals to a rite of passage was ridiculous.

"How can you compare killing a helpless two-week-old baby seal with hunting a deer?" She asked him. "The seal doesn't have a chance. Should we kill off fawns at two weeks and call it sport? The word *humane* cannot be connected to this slaughter."

To emphasize the point Tanya actually journeyed to the site of the slaughter with an API film crew. When informed that the government would not allow them to land, she stated that she wouldn't mind being arrested if it would help the cause. In her spare time she made calls and visits to her new L.A. friends and got Pamela Sue Martin and Seals and Crofts involved. Like a woman possessed, she was bound and determined to make something happen.

Not stopping with seals, Tanya also made public appearances and statements for blue whales and other endangered species. In the midst of showing a more raucous, raw side of her personality in the recording studio, she was also showing what her friends knew to be her biggest muscle, her tender heart.

Tanya had to reshape her career to reach the goals she had in mind. As much as she would have liked to spend every day of 1978 trying to save animals, she had a career that was endangered if she didn't produce a hit single and album. Still she never quit pressing her thoughts on this matter to the press. While the seals had made a huge impression on Tanya's consciousness, they hadn't done much for her career.

"Save Me" only hit the eighties on the country charts and didn't even crack the top one hundred in pop/rock. This scared the label a bit. So, even with a stack of hard rockin' numbers in the can, MCA turned to the more traditionally country "Texas When I Die" as the first release from its upcoming album. The single, even with its Nashville flavor, was shipped to both the rock and country radio stations.

With LaCosta singing the harmonies, "Texas" raced past "Save Me," and by November 1975 carried Tanya as far as the fifth position on the country charts. The flip or "B" side of "Not Fade Away, Texas" climbed to #70 on the rock charts. With "Texas" on the move it was time to ship the album.

In a sense "TNT" was real dynamite. Unlike the singles which made it up, the album sold better than any of Tanya's other general release collections. And while her greatest hits selections carried more weight, not even they could generate the talk of "TNT." This album sold for shock value as much as it did for hit potential and would give rise to the thought that Tanya was well suited for the crossover or straight rock market.

"TNT" quickly shot up the country album charts and peaked at #2. But how many people bought it out of curiosity to see what this new Tanya sounded like, as opposed to how many folks purchased it because of what they heard on the radio was unknown. What was known was that a number of hot-blooded males grabbed it for the cover art.

If listeners thought that some of Tanya's vocal inflections were suggestive, then the pictures of the artist that graced the album cover were even more suggestive. In every form of presentation "TNT" was a dramatic move toward capitalizing on Tanya's pure sex appeal. On the front cover a mike cord snaked between her legs and pulled tightly against her crotch. The look on her face indicated she was enjoying the pose a bit too much. A *Playboy* styled two-page spread folded out from the inside of the album. It showed Tanya in tight red spandex. One glance convinced her fans that she had left the flowers and frilly dresses, as well as her underwear, behind. "This is me," the photo cried out. Yet this skin-tight draping which showed every womanly curve was a radical departure from the image she had projected just a few months before. Now the tigress that always seemed to be hidden inside Tanya had jumped out carrying a handful of dynamite ready to explode.

If she and MCA wanted tongues to wag, it worked. Everybody was talking about her new look. As a matter of fact, the new look got higher reviews than the new sound. The guts of the album, the music, had been lost in the rush to see Tanya's now very grown-up body. So in a very real sense "TNT" was much more about form than substance.

The offstage innocence which had been projected in the past was now thrown out too. In venues very much different from country fairs and small town gyms, Tanya was strutting and moaning. She was bumping, grinding, jumping and moving like never before. She was raw, she was trying to be very hot, and she was generating this heat in clubs like New York's Bottom Line and L.A.'s Roxie. With each strut, with each seductive shoulder roll, it was obvious she wanted to be compared more to Tina Turner than Barbara Mandrell.

Once she had told reporters that she would never name her band because, "Elvis never did." Now as she went on stage to introduce herself to the rock crowd she changed her mind. Using the album and its hot image for inspiration, she christened her band TNT. And like her band, she exploded each and every night. The problem was the explosions didn't have direction or control. But for a while that didn't matter.

Rock crowds moaned as Tanya tossed off lewd, sexual comments. They laughed when she informed the audience, "My name is Tanya, pronounced Tan ya hide." Then to turn up the heat even more the new look and new hot act went a step further.

There was a full-page shot of a seductive Tanya advertising her new album on pages of *Hustler* magazine. The ad's lead read, "This album will make your ears hard!"

This spread may have been the beginning of the end of Tanya's rock career. Seeing his daughter surrounded by shots of very raw pornography was more than Beau could handle. He began a search to find out just who was responsible. No one in his daughter's new organization would take credit. Still he vowed that he would gain more control of her career.

As shocked as her father was, members of the press who once wondered if Tanya wouldn't do better in rock were now having second thoughts. By and large the reviewers seemed to indicate they believed that the Tanya they now observed on stage was uncomfortable and was embarrassing herself. Most thought her movements and crude remarks were forced. They wished for the good old girl who was fun, but never raw. This didn't seem natural for her.

Tanya shot back, "You can take what I think of reviewers, stick it in a paper bag and burn it." Remarks like this didn't win her any friends in the media, but it did get her attention in places that had ignored her in the past.

Playboy wrote, "Tanya Tucker, Nashville's little Levied Lolita, evanesced into America's recent hard-on for the Texas Outlaw groove and the subsequent country-rock crossover onslaught. Country Music's loss is Rock's gain."

Beau, still upset over the *Hustler* ad, was now publicly at odds with his daughter's new image. To attempt to shore up what was left of her Nashville base, he told people that contrary to what they had head, Tanya was still a sweet little girl. As her father preached, Tanya continued to project even more raw sexuality on stage.

Beau justifiably feared that she might be committing career suicide. With this in mind, he attempted to gain more control of what was going on. Many who were now a part of the new Tucker team in Los Angeles urged the singer to fire her dad claiming he was holding her back.

As long as he was there, they warned, she wouldn't become a strong rocker. Many around the recording business were now thinking of him much like Colonel Parker. Tanya might go against her father's wishes from time to time, but she still was very loyal to him. The folks in L.A. were putting the singer in a terrible spot. Of course her father was too.

In the past Beau had fought to keep her natural. It was Beau who had taken on the music establishment and kept her from having lessons of any kind. "She is a natural, she's not plastic," he had explained. He still wanted her to be natural, but he didn't really believe what he was seeing was the little girl he had known and managed now grown into a young woman. He felt it was time to put a rein on her and sell something closer to what they had sold in the past.

Tanya and her father were at opposite poles and they had distinctly different perceptions of where she should be going with her career. During this period, their battles were heated. Yet Beau had never disowned her or even stated publicly that he wished she was doing something else. He remained solidly in her corner even when he believed that the direction she was taking was wrong. He didn't walk away. And for now, in spite of what the West Coast advisors wanted, she would not walk away from him either.

Tanya figured that part of being an entertainment superstar was being an actress. When she had the opportunity to try it, she jumped in and appeared on NBC's "Amateur Night at the Dixie Bar and Grill." Tanya played a shy, small-town country singer who had frozen on stage. This was a radical departure for Tanya; she had never been still on stage. She couldn't even remember ever being frightened. Yet making the movie was fun. It also gave her a chance to plug a new tune, "I'm the Singer, You're the Song." Unfortunately the plug did nothing for the song on the pop side. It failed to crack the top one hundred. It seemed that the rock audiences might have been interested in Tanya at the beginning of her move, but they didn't really consider her anything more than a pretender. It was beginning to be obvious that she would never be welcomed on the inside.

Surprisingly, even in early 1979, despite the new raw image and the West Coast address, Tanya had enough of a country music following left to chart songs on the Nashville based charts. "I'm the Singer" lasted thirteen weeks in the top one hundred and peaked at #18. It wasn't a great showing, but it wasn't a complete washout either. But as far as MCA was concerned, the fact that the album was not producing hits on the rock side hurt Tanya's chances for a long-term commitment. Even a special nomination didn't sway them to forge on.

Admittedly it may have been shock value that earned "TNT" its early sales and notice, but it was probably Tanya's talent and fire that brought in the Grammy nomination. As had been the case with Tanya since her country music debut almost seven years before, she would be a bridesmaid rather than a bride. Still, in this case, after fighting all the controversy and surviving the year, the nomination was something positive to hang her hat on.

She later told Cynthia Fowler of the *Washington Observer Reporter,* "What happened was, the people who were supposed to be taking me from the place where I was—in country music—to the place I wanted to be—in rock music—weren't the right people.

"You can fall into the wrong hands sometimes, and that's what happened. They wanted to shock the world; me, going rock 'n' roll. I didn't want to shock the world; I wanted to spread my wings and try to experiment a little bit." It was strange indeed for a singer with a Grammy nomination to suddenly be considered dead in the water, but that is where Tanya was. Bookings were fewer, requests for interviews were down, and no one seemed to have much of an idea where to go.

Fearing that another year like the last one would kill her, Beau again took charge. The first thing he did was to fire the management team Tanya had put together to orchestrate her "experimental" move to rock. In an attempt to recoup some of the losses he hired the Scottie Brothers. They had managed Eddie Rabbit and taken the New Jersey songwriter to the top of the country music concert draw list. Beau put his faith in their hands and then pretty much walked away. Tanya's Brentwood, Tennessee, farm had grown to two thousand acres and he decided to go back there, work the horses and look for ways to invest past earnings. He felt that Tanya was now in good hands.

In their eyes it may have happened too late, but in a sense the L.A. crowd had gotten what they wanted. Daddy was gone. Yet Beau could be satisfied that he had been responsible for getting rid of what he viewed were the worst elements to come between him and his daughter's career. And while he was officially out of her professional life, he was still ready at a moment's notice to rush in and help her if she called. Financially secure, his family was still more important to him than his own time and interests.

Tanya's next album, "Tear Me Apart," hit stores in late 1980. Without the shock value of "TNT," it couldn't generate curiosity sales. It would have to be carried on the strength of the songs. Somehow Tanya singing "I Left My Heart in San Francisco" and "San Francisco (Be Sure to Wear Some Flowers in Your Hair)" didn't catch on with the fans. The release produced no hits.

Just before going into the rock scene, Tanya had pronounced herself a liberated redneck. "I have been raised with a certain sense of values and I guess I have stuck with them. I haven't tried marijuana and I wouldn't have sex with a man before I married him."

But now that she was away from Nashville, away from the influence of her family, she had more and more friends who did almost every illicit thing they could find. Tanya fell under their seductive lure. A childhood of work behind her, she jumped feetfirst into the fast lane. Soon she was drinking whiskey and scotch straight from the bottle. A decade later Tanya would tell David Hutchings of *People*, "I was the wildest thing out there. I could stay up longer, drink more and kick the biggest ass in town. I was on the ragged edge."

Tanya was soon surrounded by deadbeats she supported with her friendship and money. They hung on, laughed at her every joke, spent her cash, drank her booze and told her how great she was. They were anything but honest, and they were only loyal as long as the money, drugs or booze held out. From time to time they would turn on her for a dollar—selling a story about her wild life to the media—yet she would always forgive them, welcome them back in and pour them another drink.

One of the good things that happened during this black period was Michael Tovar. A Beverly Hills hairstylist he would turn into one of Tanya's best West Coast friends. He saw the potential in her, saw through her pain and into her heart, and realized that she needed to grow as both an entertainer and a person. Rather than bleeding her like so many of her new friends, he simply did his job and offered his faith and loyalty. He was there long after all the others had jumped ship. He listened to her when few others would. He offered honest advice. Tanya would reward his kindness and conviction by sending countless clients his way. She would also never forget him and continue to rely on his skills and his advice even after she left Los Angeles and turned her career and life around.

Still one friend or even a host of friends weren't enough. Tanya needed a hit song, a new direction for her career, some positive publicity. If she didn't get these things soon, she might just become another disappearing child star—another very public adolescent figure who had faded into oblivion because he or she couldn't make the giant step to maturity. At this point most people wouldn't bet on Tanya climbing back to the top.

"I cut a really great album," she told the press, "and nobody liked anything on it, so I said, 'I'll see ya.' "

The question now was where and when?

Chapter Eight

The Rhinestone Cowboy

I gave God a prayer and He gave me Tanya!
—Glen Campbell

A record company bio of the postrock period proudly proclaimed, "Everything's Coming Up Tanya!" Yet in all honesty it was somewhat different.

Rather than growing or moving forward, Tanya was for all practical purposes stuck in the mud. A great number of country music professionals and fans viewed her as a has-been who had rejected them. Tanya could actually "feel" the hostility whenever she made a trip back to Music City. In a sense she was being treated as if she were an unconvicted but fully accused Benedict Arnold. It was indeed a strange time.

During this period Nashville welcomed with open arms the old rockers who jumped over to country. Kenny Rogers, Jerry Lee Lewis, Conway Twitty and a host of other big-name acts, including a man named Glen Campbell, had all crossed the river to country from rock 'n' roll shores. Like a church welcoming a lifelong sinner at a revival meeting, these folks were lovingly embraced. But no one who had started in country and then jumped to the other side and tried to come back had been so welcomed. They were not to be trusted. They were sinners who had slapped the mother church in the face and disgraced its name. For them there was no salvation. In Nashville it did look like the old saying, "You can't go home again" was true.

When Tanya had turned her back on country music, country music had turned its back on Tanya. She was poison. She was dangerous. Yet what was even worse than Music City pushing her aside was that while show business in general didn't care if she had run from her roots, they didn't much want her either. In all circles Tanya seemed to be proving what had always been viewed as a fact—a child star can't grow up. While the world was looking for fresh new talent, Tanya was often seen as old hat. It was mostly her own fault. She really hadn't been ready for the jump to a new audience.

The rock experiment had failed so badly that most of the old country clubs were not interested in booking her. And unlike rock 'n' roll, country music didn't have "old-timers tours" and nostalgia shows. There really wouldn't be a place for former Music City recording sensations until Branson began to take off.

Not everything was hopeless, she still could get bookings, they just weren't the huge ones which had once come calling. She was not a headliner, but with her long list of hits and solid performances skills, she could still bring in a crowd at some casinos in Vegas as well as on the fair circuit. But for determined and driven Tanya, this was not enough.

The young woman who was once a superstar yearned for something other than being known as another female country singer who had some hits a long time ago. Unlike most other girl acts, she wanted to be known and remembered for her performance, not just holding a mike and looking fragile. When she walked on stage, she wanted to get a reaction more like Conway than Loretta. And while the fans still cheered, it wasn't as loud as it had been a few years before. Their passion seemed to be fading. This hurt more than record sales tailing off into almost nothing.

Tanya was quickly fading from the radio playlist and the magazine features. It was sad for a young woman just into her twenties to be considered a veteran past her prime. Yet this was very much the case. Many bookers wanted her, but only to open for acts that had just hit the charts for the first time a year or two before. This had to hurt. Who wants to be asked, "Didn't you used to be a star?"

Yet Tanya was still on top in one field. She could party with anyone. She was a country gal gone wild in the city. She had already become a legend on the strip. She could drink alcohol and smoke cigarettes with anyone. She knew the funniest jokes, she knew the best dance spots, and she could boogie long after everyone else was "tuckered" out. The energy which had once exploded out of her on stage, now, more often than not, was coming out at bars. Like a college kid on spring break, she seemed to be making up for lost time.

In a very real sense Tanya did have a lot of time to make up for. She had worked almost solidly from her junior high years until she moved to Los Angeles. During this period she had almost never been alone or on her own. She had been so focused on being a star and doing whatever it took to take her star higher that she had rarely gotten a chance to play. So the fact that she seemed hell-bent on welcoming many a dawn with a loud group of carefree folks seemed only natural.

Yet those who knew her well realized that Tanya was not really the man-chasing drinker they were now watching. Deep inside she was someone who would almost always rather be on the open trail in the great outdoors riding a horse or watching wild animals. They knew that she was searching for something and they hoped she found it before something tragic happened. Any fool could see that her life-style was not healthy.

"Everybody knows who I am," Tanya said when speaking about her career during this time, "they are just waiting to see what happens next." The same could be said for her private life too! What was going to happen next?

Tanya was by this time very well known in the Vegas community. Not only had she worked there on several occasions, but she had partied there too. A lot of the regular strip entertainers had worked either television specials or road shows with her. It was not unusual for her to be seen with some of the folks who headlined in the big showrooms. Who wouldn't want to party with a young woman who knew how to have fun and called a young woman named Beverly Hills her best friend.

In the spring of 1980 one of Vegas's best-known performers was in Los Angeles. On a lark and looking for a good time, he called Tanya. The man's name was Glen Campbell.

The first time Campbell and Tanya had met was at the Grand Ole Opry after one of her first appearances. At thirteen, she was star struck by the tall, thin and then very hot superstar. She even began to carry a photo of him in her billfold. Even though they had worked together on occasion after that, the relationship had never gone beyond a "Hello," or "Nice show," until Elvis's death. When Tanya had tracked down Glen to talk about the King, the two of them began to get to matters of the heart. Owing to Glen's marriage and Tanya's age, nothing more than friendship came of the relationship at that time.

Yet on this L.A. evening, with Tanya entertaining her mother at the star's beachfront condo, something clicked. Just like almost everything else in her life, the birth of her relationship with Glen was largely a matter of timing.

Campbell was married to his third wife, the former Sarah Davis. Sarah had been married to singer/songwriter Mac Davis, a good friend of Glen's, until Campbell had wooed her away from Mac. This move had stirred up the entertainment gossip mill like few things since the Eddie Fisher/Liz Taylor/Richard Burton mess on the set of *Cleopatra*. Sarah and Glen had ridden out the storm for a while, but now things seemed to be going bad. Glen was tired of his mother-in-law always hanging around, and Sarah was tired of Glen complaining. As strained as things were, it was probably not unusual for Glen to seek comfort in a quiet dinner spent with someone who could listen to him talk about his woes. The mere fact that Juanita would be with him and Tanya meant that the evening would for all appearances seem very innocent and wholesome. And so it was. The three of them got to know each other better, shared a few laughs, and then went their separate ways. And it might have never gone beyond this point if an old associate of Tanya's hadn't stepped back into the picture.

Even though he hadn't produced her in years, Buddy Killen continued to visit Tanya. Once, while on the West Coast, he picked her up and took her to a small party at Glen's California home. By this time Campbell was for the most part separated from his wife and living the life of a carefree bachelor. The sight of Killen, followed by the sexy young Tucker, brought a smile to his face. As the group sat around his large family-style room singing songs and telling stories with a half-dozen other music types, sparks began to fly. Glen couldn't take his eyes off Tanya. He found himself catering to her every whim. By the time the evening ended, Glen couldn't get the girl out of his mind.

In his 1994 autobiography *Rhinestone Cowboy,* Glen wrote of the emotions which drove him during this period of his life. "Tanya had a reputation for personal recklessness. I surprised myself by pursuing her romantically, and many friends strongly advised me against it. They told me she was an incurable party girl who was incapable of faithfulness." Yet the bottom line was that

Campbell was smitten and he didn't heed the "storm" warnings.

With friends begging him to reconsider, the rebounding Glen jumped in with both feet even though he was more than twenty years older than Tanya. Like a high school kid with a crush he rushed in without thinking of the consequences. He called her and chased her. She responded. She was looking for a man, a Southern type who spoke about the Bible but could then sin with the best of them. She liked his passion, his style, and his desire to shower her with parties and gifts. In no time the two were a much talked about show business couple.

Early on Glen was amazed and amused at how crass Tanya could be. He had rarely heard a woman who could get as earthy as a man and still maintain all of her female charms. Yet Tanya could. With both friends and the press he often referred to her as "the raunchy young broad."

Young may be the operative word too. Glen was in his midforties. He was no longer a smiling teen idol. He was an aging man who was hitting the crazy—grab for the last of youth—period of life. Tanya had so much energy, she could party for so long, she laughed so much, that she seemed to energize him. This allowed him to ignore his own age and pretend he was a kid again. He was loving every minute of it. But how long could he keep up with the dynamo without killing himself. His friends wondered.

Glen told everyone, "She is the woman I want to be with."

Since hitting the West Coast, Tanya had dated a lot, but usually only one person at a time. Even in her wildest partying days, she was loyal to the people she was with. This included the men in her life. So bringing Glen quickly on as a steady wasn't a hard adjustment. At this point there were no other challengers in the field. What probably shocked her the most was just how quickly this award-winning star fell for her. How soon he was begging her to marry him. She had never been faced with this kind of man before.

Campbell claimed that he fell harder in love with Tanya than he ever had with anyone else. He didn't just tell her this, he proudly proclaimed it to everyone. He seemed proud to show her off, take her around town, lavish time and gifts on her. "She's a great gal and I'm tired of being kicked around," he told folks. This was probably as much a slap at his last wife as it was a compliment for Tanya. But she didn't care. Tanya loved to be put on a pedestal.

Even though their relationship quickly grew, people around them really wondered if Glen had lost his mind. This simply couldn't work, they thought. The two people were much too different.

In a statement that would later come back to haunt him, Glen told both the media and friends, "I gave God a prayer and He gave me Tanya."

Sarah, his soon to be ex-wife added a sharp response, "Well, I gave God a prayer too, and He let Glen find Tanya Tucker."

Glen and Tanya didn't live together, at least not in public. Because of Glen's outward Christian values, he couldn't afford to let his fans know he was heavily involved with Tanya. Those who knew both of them well had to laugh at this notion. Still Glen's reputation for having a deep faith coupled with his family's strong and upright stature did seem to reassure those close to Tanya. Beau and Juanita seemed to accept Glen at face value. Both prayed that he was the man who could pull Tanya out of her downward personal spiral. In fact he was actually contributing to an even deeper plunge!

Even while partying with Glen, Tanya made no secret that she yearned for a strong family life and peace. She sensed that Glen's family had that, but she wondered after three failed marriages and a houseful of children if Glen could pull it off. She was smart to question just how committed he was to this institution he publicly stated was so hallowed.

Over the course of a few months, with each guesting at the other's shows, with their showing up at parties together, with their attending award presentations on each other's arm, it became obvious that the two were going to try to make this strange union work. Skeptics began to believe a little. Part of it was because Glen made Tanya sound like the best thing that had ever happened to any man.

He said that being with Tanya had encouraged him to cut back on booze and get in shape. A seemingly always smiling Campbell told anyone who would listen that now, for the very first time in his life, he was really, wholeheartedly in love. It was a miracle!

What may have been the real miracle was that it lasted for fifteen months. For Tanya, whose recent personal life had been like a trip through the outskirts of hell, being with Campbell made those past days look like a stroll in the park. Glen smoked and drank as much as Tanya, and he also had a history of drug abuse. While claiming that being together was a factor in both of them cleaning up their bad habits, they were getting into cocaine in a bigger way than ever. They spent a great many days stoned.

There were days and nights filled with all kinds of passion, and not all of it was healthy. Fights, very loud and very physical, were the rule, not the exception. Glen would later claim that Tanya could deliver a blow like a man. Yet, when they weren't fighting or loving, when they were clean and sober and when they were simply singing together, their harmonies were rich and there seemed to be magic in the air.

Tanya worked with Campbell on an HBO special,

Mississippi Days, Southern Nights, which amounted to little more than a concert from Harrah's in Reno. They looked and sounded great together. She also traveled to Europe with Campbell to work on a television special from Monte Carlo.

"It is incredible the way our voices blend together," she would brag. "Glen and I both feel the same way about music. He's been very fortunate in his career and he's helping me a lot in mine."

Tanya needed some help because her recording career was stuck and going nowhere. The exposure on Glen's shows helped, but what she really needed was a hit record. To find the right formula she jilted L.A. and headed back to an increasingly hostile Nashville. There she met with old time friend and producer Jerry Crutchfield. She told him about Campbell, "Our voices blend so well it is almost sinful not to work together." Crutchfield listened and agreed and put the two together in the studio. But much more than record duets, he wanted to get his girl back in touch with the kind of material he thought she needed to be recording. Back with Jerry, Tanya seemed to be comfortable again with herself and her music.

"Country music has a feel," she said at the time. "You can't put a rock player in my band if he doesn't know country. They can't play it if they can't feel it. Believe me, it's not as easy as some people might think." Nor would be coming up with a new batch of hits.

The new album would be called "Dreamlovers." No one had to guess who the other lover besides Tanya was, but what was in question was whether Tanya was going to come back and do some real country music. Crutchfield assured them that she was.

"The bottom line is to have quality songs," the producer explained, intimating that he felt the West Coast folks had given the singer something but quality. Then he added, "Tanya is strong in the country marketplace, but she is also a young, contemporary person. She looks and sounds contemporary in a way that doesn't detract from her country appeal. In other words, I am going to get this woman in touch with her roots and show you people that she can still sing with country music's best."

Her "Pecos Promenade" carried this old country feel and was an important part of the sound track to the widely successful Burt Reynolds movie *Smokey and the Bandit 2*. On the charts for fourteen weeks in the summer of 1980, "Pecos Promenade," complete with Glen Campbell's voice on one verse, peaked at #10. Tanya was back in a fashion, but for how long? Besides was it the fans wanting Tanya that pushed her back into prominence on the charts? Or was it the success of the Burt Reynolds/Jackie Gleason movie combined with Campbell's presence on the cut? In retrospect there is no doubt that the movie helped, but "Promenade" was a strong song and Tanya's vocal presentation sold it well. Even without the movie it would probably have been a hit. As far as Glen's help, it probably did not have nearly as great an impact as most people still believe. After all, Glen was not anywhere close to the top at this time.

Contrary to the way that some remember it, Campbell's career was nothing to brag about during this time. It had been three years since he had a song which had climbed into the top ten. His only major hit during this period, "Southern Nights," had become more of a swan song than something on which he could ascend to the zenith of country music. He had become a personality with enough hits to host television specials and get work as a Las Vegas headliner, but he was no longer a superstar. And unlike his friend, Johnny Cash, who was also an Arkansas native, he hadn't built impressive enough numbers to be considered a legend. Odds were that he was never going to be inducted into the Country Music

Association's Hall of Fame. He was, in a sense, becoming a "has-been."

So in many ways recording with Tanya brought Glen as much if not more than the teaming with Glen brought Tanya. Her audience was young and aggressive, on the cutting edge of a new country/rock scene. Campbell's was middle-age, or at least very soon to be, and growing more conservative by the second. They weren't buying products like they had during his productive crossover years. Glen needed an injection of energy to make him appear younger than his own middle-age years, and keeping company with Tanya could prove that there was still a "tiger in his tank."

With Crutchfield at the controls Tanya and Glen tried duet magic with Bobby Darin's classic "Dream Lover." It was a pretty solid cut, yet the song just languished on the charts for six weeks in mid-1980, peaking at a mediocre #59. Then, as if to prove that she didn't need Glen to reestablish herself on the country music charts, two months later Tanya hit the #4 spot with "Can I See You Tonight." For all apparent purposes it was Tanya who was selling herself. Apparently all she needed was a producer who understood her sound and how to work with her to bring out the best.

MCA had learned its lesson at trying to make big books off the two, but Glen's label, Capitol, hadn't. The label tried its own hand at publicity to sell the two as a duet team and in April 1981 shipped "Why Don't We Just Sleep on It Tonight." Capitol executives probably should have slept on it before they spent the money to ship the song. It stayed a tortuous four weeks on the charts and never hit any higher than #85.

With the success she had earned on her last solo single, Tanya should have been ready to ride a wave of follow-ups even higher. Yet that didn't happen. She released three singles in 1981, "Love Knows We Tried," "Should I Do It," and "Rodeo Girls." None of them rode the charts for more than eight weeks and only "Love Knows We Tried" cracked the top forty. "Love" hit that spot and quickly fell out of sight. What happened to the comeback which had looked so strong? The answer was her coupling with Glen Campbell and what it was doing to both her life and her reputation.

By early summer 1980, Glen was talking marriage both privately and publicly. A middle-age man who had just dumped his third wife was creating a scandal in the process. He probably should have kept a lower dating profile. He certainly didn't need to be fooling around with a very young woman who was still perceived by most of the American public as a child. Nevertheless, he pushed forward, all the while spouting speeches about wanting to marry Tanya because it was the right thing to do. Even when he was in the midst of a wildly passionate romance, he told the press he had to marry Tanya. Most people didn't buy it, but a political party did.

Glen's conservative stance garnered the two a chance to sing the national anthem at the Republican National Convention in July. They had both previously trumpeted their support of Ronald Reagan, and it was for his cause they blended their voices on July 14, 1980. The members of the Grand Ole Party were pleased to have the two stars singing their praises. What they didn't know was that while their own platform and rhetoric was announcing a new war on drugs, while the future first lady was pushing her "just say no," concept, both Tanya and Glen were as high as a kite on cocaine as they sang "The Star Spangled Banner." Such were the inconsistencies in their lives. They projected one thing but seemed to live something far different. Most of the fault for this had to be placed on Glen. He was the hypocrite. One thing Tanya had rarely done was not admit and take responsibility for her own actions. Besides the drugs and the sex, there was a stronger undercurrent which was slowly ripping the two from each other.

In front of the curtain they professed unity and harmony, but behind the spotlight Tanya and Glen competed. Glen seemed concerned that people thought that Tanya was the bigger star. He took pains to point out his long list of hits and awards. In his mind she was an opening act, and he was the closer. He wanted everyone to know that.

He also didn't like and couldn't understand why Tanya didn't seem to mind always being in the public eye. She would even talk about their fights and disagreements to the press. Glen believed that Tanya even loved and thrived on bad publicity. What he often failed to consider was that almost all of her bad publicity came from dating a man old enough to be her father—a man who had been around a few times before. At this point Glen *was* her bad publicity. And he was also contributing to her bad habits.

Together the two got into heavy cocaine use. They used so much that at one time or another Glen thought it was going to kill him. While under the influence their fights were hotter and their behavior even more bizarre. She set off firecrackers in Glen's house and they went to tennis great Yvonne Goolagong's wedding in bathing trunks and bikini. They didn't seem to care what people thought. In many cases they might not have known or realized what they were doing.

Glen tossed Tanya a birthday bash in 1980 at L.A.'s Bistro that reportedly cost sixty thousand dollars. That evening he said that he was "dating one of the finest female talents that God lets draw breath." Was it Glen or the drugs talking? He friends didn't know.

As the days went by, the drug use grew worse and the relationship grew even more strange. Glen's friends blamed Tanya for this heavy drug use. Tanya's friends blamed Glen. It didn't matter who was at fault, they both seemed to urge each other on. The drugs even began to affect their shows. On stage they weren't sharp, and when they tried to be funny, they weren't. Yet by and large the public didn't know about this side of their life together. Most assumed it was just stuff the scandal sheets made up. Before long it would be public record.

Glen viewed the sober Tanya as sweet and the high Tanya as mean and selfish. One would have to question if this fit because Glen was usually high when Tanya was and this meant that he would have been judging the young woman based on a mind that was heavily under the influence. There is one thing that was known. The relationship was driven by sex.

Tanya would say, "He's the horniest man I have ever known."

Maybe this was what Glen was thinking of when he told *People,* "There's a bond there I'm not going to break . . . We're at peace when we're together." In all honesty, it was more like war.

Tanya was much more honest when she informed the national magazine, "Who knows what will happen? Tomorrow I may run off with Mac Davis." No one checked with Mac or Sarah Davis to see if they saw the humor and irony in Tanya's view.

At Christmas the two were together skiing in the Canadian Rockies and making wedding plans. If one were to believe what the male half was saying in public, Tanya was the all-American girl. Meanwhile it could be quickly established that Glen was a forty-four-year-old grandfather. He was certainly no virgin!

"Our love is magic," Glen was quoted in the *Star.* "It is a gift from God."

Tanya added, "When two people are singing of love, people can tell whether or not it's phony. But we really feel it and it shows."

As a follow-up the Rhinestone Cowboy may have

taken this fairy tale a little too far when he added,
"When we're together on stage, well, it is like the Bible
says, if one falls, the other is there to pick them up. Just
knowing she's there makes me more loose and more
creative." He was loose, but he was no longer very creative.

For months Glen had been asking Tanya to marry him
and Tanya had kept turning him down and putting him
off. Finally the couple set and announced a Valentine's
Day ceremony. The wedding never happened. The often
brutal relationship simply couldn't last the six weeks until the ceremony.

Tanya and Glen hit bottom first during the filming of
the CBS special *Country Comes Home*. Glen checked
into a local hospital after a heavy drug binge and decided to walk away from the codependent relationship.
If the entertainer thought cocaine was hard to give up, it
was nothing compared to trying to take himself off
Tanya.

One night when Glen was working a hundred miles
away from Tanya's Louisiana date, he decided he had to
be with her. He rushed to her side as quickly as he could
and she welcomed him back. While Glen may have been
simply turned-on by Tanya—she was his sex drug—she
seemed to really love him. She wanted him for more
than just a few minutes. This may have begun a fight
that would make national press.

Tanya would later claim in a lawsuit that Glen
knocked out two of her teeth in that Louisiana fight. In
his 1994 book Glen claimed it was Tanya who always
attacked him. This night had been no different. He tried
to paint himself as the victim, a man who had been
abused and was fighting back. Yet if that were the case,
why did he drive so far and go to so much trouble just to
get to this very small woman's room?

Glen seemed to intimate to his friends and family that
he kept coming back because he was scared what Tanya

would do if he walked out of her life. He claimed that she had even tried to commit suicide once by cutting her wrists. Like so many of Campbell's claims, Tanya dismissed them as completely untrue.

Glen also seemed to want to rescue Tanya from her own family. Glen believed that Tanya spent too much time around her family and that it was unhealthy. This was also his reasoning for breaking up with his last wife. He couldn't seem to handle in-laws.

Even after the Louisiana affair, Glen continued to chase Tanya and she continued to let him back into her life. He finally broke it off while she was performing at The Nugget in Reno. He used the fact that her family was always surrounding her as one of the excuses. Then he claimed that she had been unfaithful. Tanya swore that there had never been anyone but him. She even begged him to come back to her.

It was May, just over a year after the "Romance of a Lifetime" had begun, and the now bitter Glen walked out. But he left himself with a huge problem. Tanya was booked on a European tour with him. Rather than pay her off or take her with him, he simply replaced her with Kaye Starr. This move would cost Tanya a huge amount of money in lost revenue from the canceled tour with no time to set up alternate dates in the United States. So, if revenge was his motive, when Glen had jilted Tanya, he had done it right. It hurt her almost as much as those times he had beaten her. Still she didn't lash out at him.

In a very generous reaction, she told everyone who would give her an interview that she still had feelings for the man. Even though he had stormed out, put a huge hole in her business, and all but ruined her reputation and life, she still loved him.

On her own she flew to England and tried to put it back together. It was a wasted trip, the young woman whom Glen had recently called his only true love—the girl he had asked God for—had been replaced by a pretty young dancer he had met on a blind date. In this case a love that was to last forever ended a few years short. Heartbroken, Tanya returned home.

"I am desperately in love with Glen," Tanya told all those around her, "but I guess he wants no part of me even though I'd lay down my life for him."

For Tanya getting rid of Glen would prove to be an excellent move. The tabloids had made a field day of the May-October romance, and the life-style the two of them had given in to was far worse than what she had been living before. For her own personal well-being she needed out.

From a career standpoint it was good it was over too. Being with Glen on stage and on records had not helped her at all. The audiences for their music were much too dissimilar. The two performers were from different generations and had two vastly different career goals. Tanya wanted to go higher. Meanwhile, Glen just wanted to find a way to regain lost stardom while holding onto what he had. One of them was still hungry, the other fat and satisfied.

Who was hurt the most? It was probably Tanya. She would be pushed into a downward spiral because of the time she took away from her own career to work with Glen. It would be a while before she could put it all back together, and during that time she would struggle to regain her old fire and passion, as well as her self-respect. Most thought she never would come back from her days and nights spent with "The Rhinestone Cowboy."

- Chapter Nine -

It Doesn't Feel Right

During the fifteen months I dated Tanya, I got as much press as I had during my entire thirteen-year career.

— *Glen Campbell*

*I*n a sense with this one statement Glen Campbell admitted the real power of being Tanya Tucker's man. He may have also been alluding to his lack of press after he split with Tanya. The fact was the reporters still followed her, but he was pretty much left alone. His career as a record seller was also on the downhill slide. It would be three years before he broke out of the slump, and then he would manage only a #4 with "A Lady Like You." Within ten years of their breakup Campbell was no longer releasing singles and he would never again have a #1.

Meanwhile, Tanya's days with MCA were soon to be history. The Campbell affair and reports of the bizarre behavior that went with it had seemingly driven the final spike into her career. Many in the business had already written her off as a child star, many others who had allowed her the chance to grow up had given up on her during her rock period, and those who had somehow stuck with her through these two periods, couldn't see their way clear now. MCA was among them.

Child stars often spend most of their adult life searching for the adult in them. Their identity is so linked in the minds of their audience as a child, that they are not allowed to ever grow up. Pat Boone once said of Elvis's death, it might be just as well he died at forty-two because no one "could imagine or accept an old Elvis." By the same token would anyone ever accept or love an adult Tanya? Was she dead in the water? Was Tanya on life-support? Should someone have just pulled the plug and let her fade away.

Logic would say yes, but the woman herself would say no. She was hurt, she had been misled, she had even been misused, but she was not ready to give up. She was a fighter, a young woman with her father's ability to roll with the punches and get back up. She would not give up on herself or those around her. She may have been radically bent, leaning at a huge angle, but she wasn't broken.

"Everything you live makes you who you are," she told the press as she began to look for new avenues of adventure. She vowed that she would be back on the charts and headlining big shows. Yet for the moment, she just needed some time to figure out how she wanted to do it and, more importantly, just who she was.

One of the first things she tried was acting in a serious film. *Urban Cowboy,* released in 1980, had been a huge hit. It had made white-collar America sit up and notice country music. The film had seemingly brought a new market to the Nashville sound. The words of a soon to be released song from country's reigning queen, Barbara Mandrell, pretty much summed up the thoughts of the Music City establishment as they watched millions of Americans rush out to buy boots and cowboy hats, "I was country when country wasn't cool."

Tanya had been there, she had been cool once, but for the moment she wasn't considered to even be country anymore by industry insiders. She had jumped ship. Now her best way to get back might be to get involved in a motion picture that glorified the very industry which seemed to have no place for her.

Hard Country would not be nearly as successful as

Urban Cowboy, but it would be a movie that would be remembered. The reason for that status was a strong performance by a Hollywood newcomer, Kim Basinger. This was the part that would help make her a star. It and an appearance in *Playboy* made her an actress to be noted and a sex-symbol to be remembered. For Tanya, who played a background role very well, it was a chance to watch and evaluate herself on the big screen. While the calls for really big important parts didn't roll in, she showed promise. That was something to hold onto, and because her ego had recently taken such a great beating, it was something she needed too.

"Right after Glen and I broke up," she admitted while recalling those days, "I went through a lot of sickness and tension. I realized I had not done the right thing and that I had given away more than I wanted to of my independence. I gave much more than I took." Tanya certainly didn't plan to ever do that again.

In a very real sense Tanya had to have been in a state of shock. The days with Campbell were draining. Still in public she managed to keep a strong front. She didn't look weak or vulnerable.

She was tired of being asked about the affair, but she still didn't lash out at either the press or her former love. She would say, almost as a plea to the man himself, "Still there is more good in him [Glen] than bad."

When all anybody wanted to talk to her about was her ex and her record company was no longer pushing her stuff, there simply wasn't much left for her to do. While she wasn't broke, she didn't have a great deal of money either. Her father had invested his management percentage well, and he had purchased property for her that offered a parachute, but the bank accounts that she used on a daily basis for her partying and playing were dwindling down to very little.

Rebounding from Glen and having little direction in

her career also probably lead to Tanya being linked with a long list of different men. Some were little more than friends, a few were flings, and with an even smaller number she had special feelings. But none on the list came close to sweeping her off her feet and making her want to embrace a wedding day.

One of her "friends" who got the most press was Dean Dillon. At twenty-seven he was a very good-looking Nashville musician. While Dillon never climbed into the top twenty on the Billboard charts on his own, he did score several times as a songwriter. Maybe the best of these was "Lying in Love With You" for Jim Ed Brown and Helen Cornelius.

Dean and Tanya worked together on some shows. They always claimed to be friends, but the tabloids indicated there was much more there. If it was anything more than a friendship, it was something less than a fling too. With Glen so closely in her background, with the lessons that have gone along with that former relationship, Tanya had good reason not to want to tie herself down to one person. Soon after Dillon and Tucker split, Tanya also left the country tour circuit. With no real hits, with no prospect of MCA wanting to cut any more records, she felt she didn't have the support and backing to go on. She didn't want to admit that she might be washed up, but the fact was it sure did appear that she was headed that way.

In 1982 the little money that was left in her own accounts finally ran out. She had partied a great deal of it away, but her own generosity had killed her time and time again. If a friend wanted a new dress, she bought it for them. If a bunch of folks joined her at a grill, she picked up the tab. She was always making sure those around had something special from her. She just loved making others feel good. So it was not unusual that during her last days in Los Angeles she used her rent and food money to pay for a friend's cancer treatments. It seemed that the sick friend had no money or insurance. As she signed the check, it really seemed like it was all over.

While Tanya had been largely managed by West Coast types during this period, her father hadn't stayed completely out of the picture. He still had a hand in a few things and he managed to keep informed as to what was going on in her life. Sensing that something had to be done to help his girl, Beau came to Los Angeles, paid off her bills, squared her accounts and helped her pack her bags. With very little fanfare and no press coverage, Tanya moved back to Nashville. But she didn't stay long. She still didn't feel comfortable there. Besides Music City didn't offer much in the way of career opportunity.

In a move that surprised many of her friends and some of her family, she flew to New York and enrolled in Lee Strasberg's acting school in New York. She had been one of only four of seven hundred applicants who had been accepted for the spring and summer workshop. It was a huge honor and should have done a great deal for the young woman's self-confidence.

Strasberg had been responsible for transforming many average actors into big-time stars. Marilyn Monroe had used her experience at his school to go back to the West Coast and land significantly meatier roles. Many had believed that the school had made her a star. If you made it through this school, it was believed, there was a good chance for you to get a solid shot at working in film and television for a long time.

In a sense, Tanya had shown pretty good instincts on film. This seemed to be a solid career move. It allowed her to change her reputation and be taken seriously. It was a rare opportunity to study with the best. It would also give her a shot to be remembered as more than just a former child star and country music singer. After only two weeks she left. Just like in high school, Tanya dropped out. She was still in a hurry, she had been since she was eight-years-old, and at the Strasberg school it was taking too long. She wanted a quicker career fix. She didn't want to wait years.

For a while she stayed on in the Big Apple. While there she got caught up with another former young star who had become a tabloid regular. Andy Gibb had just been very publicly dumped by Victoria Principal. For a brief time Gibb turned to Tanya. It didn't last long. Besides Andy, the singer in search of a career path was also linked with the likes of boxer Gerry Cooney. Gerry had just been dumped by Larry Holmes. He almost lasted longer with the heavyweight champ than he did with Ms. Tucker.

Soap opera star, Ben Thomas, from "The Doctors" was another fling or flame, depending upon who was calling the shots. He and Tanya met on a Nashville-based talk show he hosted. She spent a part of the summer after Glen hitting clubs and Nashville hot spots with good-looking Thomas. Then, without warning, the actor dumped Tanya for one of his old girlfriends.

A handsome skier, Peter Underwood was another beau. Jim Kelly, who was already famous as a great quarterback, was then called into the game. He would soon become a bench warmer. Tanya was also linked with Don Johnson. They met when they worked together in two television movies Tanya signed to do, *Dixie Bar and Grill* and *The Rebels*. At first she was put off by Johnson's ego, but after a night in a restaurant at Venice, California, they hit it off and became good friends. She described his talent as almost "spiritual." But spiritual or not, she couldn't maintain her interest in Johnson either. He joined the others on the sidelines.

By and large all these relationships left Tanya lonely and blue. She wanted more than temporary affection. What she really wanted was a career.

In 1982 she took a shot at a pretty substantial acting

A young Tanya performs in front of an adoring crowd.
(© *Alan L. Mayor*)

Tanya in Lawton, Oklahoma in 1994, showing off a new look and a new show. (© *Vicki Houston*)

Left: A young Tanya in 1982, trying to climb back into the spotlight at a Nashville television taping. (© *Vicki Houston*)

Below: In 1985 the confidence was coming back, and no one in country was as sexy. (© *Vicki Houston*)

Tanya with old Wilcox, Arizona hero, Western star Rex Allen and her own brother Don at a benefit for West Texas Rehab Center. (© *Vicki Houston*)

In 1989, Tanya was almost ready to deliver when she and sister LaCosta teamed up at a Fan Fair booth. (© *Vicki Houston*)

Glen was saying that "God sent me Tanya." In retrospect their relationship was more hell than heaven.
(© *Vicki Houston*)

Tanya is great in the saddle and her love for horses has been passed on to her son. (© *Vicki Houston*)

Tanya doesn't mind sharing the spotlight with her daughter, but she isn't sure she wants her in the business. (© *Vicki Houston*)

Tanya's look evolved to elegant when she hosted the 1992
TNN Music City News Country Awards show.
(© *Vicki Houston*)

She might be a "tough as nails" businesswoman, but Tanya has a soft spot when it comes to animals and children.
(© *Vicki Houston*)

role in the made-for-television movie *Georgia Peaches*. She costarred with Dirk Benedict of *"The A-Team"*. Tanya played a singer who went back to Nashville and got caught up with a stolen car, spies and undercover operations. Mainly it was a chance to have fun, gain some needed exposure and make some much needed money. For a while it brought her back to Nashville, but she really questioned whether she wanted to go back to Music City for good. In many ways it still seemed like a hostile place to her. People still seemed to look down at her.

Yet, not everything was completely bleak. MCA had released a live album in 1982. "Live" proved that Tanya still had it together when she was performing in front of a real audience. But the album's very average sales coupled with the fact Tanya really wasn't on the road much anymore, didn't push MCA to have any more faith in her. "Cry," her final single for the label lasted only one month on the charts and died not long after the singer's twenty-fourth birthday. It was her swan song for MCA, but she wasn't exactly disappearing. Besides her work in telemovies and her romantic liaisons carried almost weekly by the tabloids, she was still managing to stay somewhat in the public eye. And if anyone knew the importance of staying visible, it was Tanya!

She was seen with television's Landers sisters at a brunch for the one hundredth show of "Entertainment Tonight." The media caught up with her in New York lighting up flashbulbs with Cindy Gibb of "Search for Tomorrow" at the premier of the Christopher Atkins movie *Pirate Movie*. She also was tracked down as she partied most of the night at Studio 5X. Other "journalists" spotted her at various New York discos including Xenon. Whether it was in a miniskirt, a tight sweater or leather pants, Tanya was still standing out. She might have been off the charts, but she certainly was still trying to hold onto her celebrity status. And this "press" worked to her advantage time and time again. When bookers or casting directors were trying to find someone to fill a slot, Tanya's publicity kept her on the front burner even if her career didn't. They couldn't help but notice the seemingly professional jet-setter. And the stories kept coming.

In 1982 she was sued by Steve M. Wallack for $3 million for failure to bring him on as road manager. He stated that the position had been promised to him. Nothing of significance came from this bit of bad publicity, except for more inches of ink.

Tanya, who was one of country music's better actors, was signed for a guest shot as a rock singer in the CBS drama "Downtown." Not long after that she made her banker happy by agreeing to a six-figure contract to open for Gabe Kaplan at the Aladdin. While most of Nashville may have had its blinders on, the fact was that even with everything going against her, Tanya could still produce.

As the *Dallas Morning News* would observe, "Even with a cold, Tanya Tucker is hot." The *Morning News* was not the only organization to notice either. Arista Records, a company which didn't dabble in country music, saw some potential in Ms. Tucker. The mere fact that they weren't a part of the Nashville establishment is probably why they decided to take a risk with her.

Arista assigned "wunderkind," David Malloy to produce the new project. He was informed that his assignment was to find out who and what Tanya Tucker is. Is she a has-been country artist ready to again break out, or is she a rock star whose shine dimmed even before she took off? Arista and Malloy really couldn't decide. They opted for country, but they just didn't have the ability or insight of Sherrill or Crutchfield.

For the first time in her career Tanya was visibly trying to get away from the female Elvis thing. She was now concentrating on finding and releasing real country songs. She was taking a much more active role in picking out her stuff and choosing what to put on the market. She had written, along with Eddie Raven, what would become the new album's title cut, "Changes." The song not only identified what she hoped would be her own change of fortune and direction, but examined what went wrong with her affair with Glen Campbell. The cut was both painful and haunting. It was also an important statement for Tanya to make. She was honestly explaining that she was trying to cope with what had happened to her, the mistakes she had made over the past few years. She was trying to get her house in order. But would anyone listen or care?

With an album and single to promote Tanya hit the country circuit again. In most cases the dates didn't pay as much as they once had and she was usually not the headliner of the multiple bills. Still she was Tanya Tucker and she was hit at every stop with reporters. The problem was that they wanted to talk more about Glen Campbell than the direction she was now headed. Still, always the trooper, Tanya winced and pushed ahead.

During a stop in Winnipeg, Canada, she looked back over her early career and told writer Randal McIlroy, "It could always be better. There's a lot of people I would not have worked with if I'd known what they were really like before, but I've just gotten down to basics now."

When he pressed about Campbell and the tabloids, she honestly replied, "You've got to be real strong about those kinds of things (bad press). I'm trying to make a living like everybody else. I've tried to do the best I could with my career. You're going to make mistakes and you're going to make changes that maybe you shouldn't have. But I'd probably do it all over again."

As the writers and others found out, Tanya wasn't going to pass the buck or lay the blame of her career decline on anyone else. She also wasn't going to admit that singing rock was a complete mistake. She still wanted to be known as an honest woman who couldn't be comfortably placed in any niche.

"I don't really like to be categorized," she strongly interjected that evening. "My roots are in country music, that's where I started from. You have to start from somewhere to go somewhere, and I'm sure I'll always be country music. I'll go down singing country." Still she hadn't and wouldn't close the door on other forms of music. Before she was a country singer, she was a singer. Period!

As the weeks back on the road began to take their toll, and the questions about Glen Campbell kept coming up, Tanya seemed to grow more reconciled to the fact that no one was going to judge her on what she was doing now. They didn't care about "Changes." All they wanted to know was the old gossip. It was frustrating. She couldn't prove herself because no one was really listening to her. This would have broken a weaker person. Somehow she rode it out.

Even though she was very hurt by the Nashville community's cold shoulder, she didn't allow that to come out in the press. As a matter of fact, she seemed to understand why they felt like they did. In a sense, she had jilted them for a city with more money and more power. In the face of the shunning she was receiving from many of those who had once been so happy to have their picture made with her a few years before, she called moving back to Music City "a healing experience." Still, she admitted that working with the industry itself was harder than ever. It seemed to have gotten so political. She was mad at the pecking order in song releasing, the lawyers who spent so much time and got so much money and seemed to do so little, and the people who made big money but didn't seem to ever do their jobs.

That last sling was probably meant for the public relations and promotional people at Arista. They were putting out a product but not promoting it. They were just letting it sit there. Tanya knew she couldn't compete without help, and she didn't seem to be getting any. It was almost like they wanted her to fail. But rather than give up, she tried to get more involved. She wanted to educate them and show them what needed to be done to sell records in country music. Even in the face of a complete lack of support from these folks, she wanted to give them a second chance. In a very real sense she knew that a second chance and maybe a last chance was what this label was giving her.

She advised Arista against releasing "Shame on the Moon" and "Until You're Mine" because they were just too rock oriented. She definitely wanted to come full circle to her country roots and make sure that radio stations and fans realized it. She needed the company to promote her that way. They listened but didn't act on the star's advice. All they seemed interested in doing was mailing out a few cuts so they could say they tried, then move on.

Arista released three singles during their year with Tanya. The first, "Feel Right," landed on the charts right after Thanksgiving in 1983 and did pretty well. It took Tanya to #10, the first time she had been there since "Can I See You Tonight," some three years before. It should have been a signal for Arista to begin a big publicity push. Unfortunately, because of a lack of experience in the country music field or a simple change of heart on Tanya, they didn't pick up on it. Tanya's next two releases, shipped with very little support, were "Changes" and "Baby I'm Yours." The latter, a cover of the old Barbara Lewis pop hit, managed only moderate success. It peaked at #22. "Changes" only managed a #41. Once again it appeared that Tanya was on a downward spiral.

Though is probably had very little to do with Tanya,

the "Changes" album also didn't move off store shelves like Arista had desired. In some cases their promotion was so poor it never got to store shelves to begin with. In most cases it was buried in the back of the record bins. So, just when it seemed like Tanya was beginning to get a feel for the road again, just when it seemed the old concert fire was back, Arista put an end to their marriage. They dumped Tanya almost as quickly as Glen Campbell had.

"She must be hard to get along with," some insiders observed as Arista cut her loose.

"She is out of control. She can't be tamed," others offered.

Yet in this case none of those things seemed to be true. Tanya may have screwed up when she participated in the move to rock, but she had very little to do with her failure at Arista. As a matter of fact, she worked hard at this professional marriage. It was the label that hadn't pulled its weight.

Looking back over her rocky first comeback year, she told *Country Sound Round-Up* in 1984, "People who are successful are said to be hard to get along with or are called bitchy or this or that. But usually the reason they're that way is that they want it done right, and they are tired of people tellin' them what to do." Tanya could have added—particularly people who don't have any idea as to what they are trying to do!

Tanya was also sick of people who were pointing fingers at her family and blaming them for her downfall. One of the most famous voices supporting this view had been Glen Campbell. She was no longer going to let this ridicule go without a response.

"Everybody thinks the family's been in the way of my career," she lashed out. "But that's not so. The family's really what kept it together. It's the professionals that have screwed it up. I'm going to stick with my family, me and my dad mainly. If it weren't for him, I wouldn't be here."

But where was here? Tanya herself wasn't really sure. She knew that she was in a period where she was trying to find herself. As a matter of fact she had been there for almost seven years. In many ways she didn't seem to be any closer to understanding just who the adult Tanya Tucker really was.

"The transition's rough," she observed to *Country Sound Round-Up.* But she intimated that even if she didn't have a recording contract, she wasn't ready to give up. "I'm still going through it (her search for her place in the industry). I think I will continue to do that throughout my career. Unless you get so huge that it finally doesn't matter what you do, you can't say, 'Hey no matter what I do, I'm going to do fine. Even if it's a mistake, it's gonna sell.' " Right now everything she had done seemed to matter.

While Tanya had been cut loose, country music seemed to be worshipping at the feet of another woman who had started young and was being managed by her father. Barbara Mandrell was now country music's biggest star. She was the one who had scored with her own network television show. She was the first woman to win the CMA's Entertainer of the Year award twice. She was the female who was setting the trends. And what a beautiful talent she was.

With country music and its fans now embracing a woman who was a "straight arrow"—a woman who seemed to be as pure as the driven snow and who had just won a Grammy for a religious album, a woman who won "Mother of the Year" awards, played softball and had mastered a dozen different instruments, a woman whom the scandal sheets could hit with absolutely nothing—was there any room left for someone like Tanya?

The "Changes" album was supposed to be the vehicle Tanya drove back to stardom. It broke down before it left the dealership. Looking around at the "new" country, Tanya now seemed strangely out of step. She was a rebel without a cause in a world that had turned its back on the rebels.

Still, even without a label, she kept pushing. And each night, as she ran through her long list of now "old" hits, she watched the applause grow a little less enthusiastic. Ending her show with her only hit off the "TNT" album, "Texas (When I Die)," she seemed to be admitting it too.

Texas crowds were still welcoming their native daughter and hell-raiser, but having Tanya welcomed to Heaven seemed much more likely than having open arms greet her in Nashville or on country music playlists. For all practical purposes it looked as though "The Texas Tornado" was running out of wind.

Chapter Ten

Hitting Bottom

My bad reputation has done wonderful things for me.

—Tanya Tucker

*T*anya Tucker was just twenty-four years old when MCA retired her. A year later Arista cut her loose. For the first time in over a decade she was not wanted by any of the major labels. They no longer thought she could sell a product. In the age of rising groups like Alabama and young up-and-coming females like Reba McEntire, Tanya was old hat. Some were even looking at her as if she were from the same generation as Kitty Wells and Patsy Montana. It wasn't unusual for the press and public to point to her and say something like, "Boy, back when she was young, she was really something!"

The stark reality of their statements seemed to rarely click in focus. The new kid on the block, Reba McEntire was four years older than Tanya. Almost all the new wave of female acts had been born before "The Texas Tornado." Of course most disc jocks didn't even know who "The Texas Tornado" was. More often than not, Tanya was now just "T." And this very singular nickname seemed to be a throwback to her female Elvis days. After all, the King's friends often called him "E." And in a very real sense, both of the entertainers might just as well have been dead. Neither were cutting any new material.

For Tanya it was frustrating. She didn't want to be

considered old news. So she tried to explain to people that just because she had been singing half her life, she was still a young woman. She argued that most country music acts didn't even score a major hit or a Grammy nomination until they were her age. Yet no one seemed to listen.

To emphasize that she still had the drive it took to come back and land on the top she would often list her goals to reporters. "I want to write more songs. I want to write a couple of movies, do Broadway, I want to do a musical film. I want to write a film with Julio Iglesias. I think he is going to be a very major star." But no one seemed to take her seriously. And there were valid reasons.

In both photos and person she looked older than her years. Some of her fans who actually knew her age thought that this woman looked too old, too used-up to be Tanya Tucker. She certainly wasn't a child star anymore. In many circles she wasn't even considered a star. But like an over-the-hill fighter, she was still out there plugging, looking for her second wind. If she found it, she had the confidence, even though it was beginning to wane, that she could once again get to the top. Yes, these were tough days.

Tanya would later refer to these times: "A few years ago I was always in a haze, I was always numb." The fact was that she didn't feel right about performing. Her drive was not there. She was struggling to find direction and goals. "I just didn't feel anything but the pain."

A part of the pain was still centered around Glen Campbell. She simply couldn't believe that he had hurt her the way he had. She also couldn't believe how quickly he had forgotten her and gotten on with his life. When he spoke of her it was more like he was describing surviving an illness than looking back on a period of time he had shared with a woman he once claimed he loved like no other.

"Why does everyone have to mention Glen Campbell, Glen Campbell?" Tanya at times seemed outraged at the questions. "Why does everyone have to mention that sucker every time a story is written about me?" She was in pain, and it showed.

Hurting was something that Tanya was now getting real good at. She now knew that in a very real sense Campbell had used her faith and trust and then thrown her away when he found she was a bit more than he could handle. Yet she was still having a hard time believing that he had never loved her. He had told her he loved her so many times. And she had learned from the example of her parents, who had been married almost forty years, that when you tell someone you love them, it is supposed to be forever. If Tanya felt used, she should have. The press was feeding off her pain now. It was seeing her hurt that brought them out to her.

Even though Glen had moved on and gotten married again, the media egged the ragged female star on about him. When pressed Tanya admitted she longed for Campbell. Yet what she might have been yearning for just as much was a sense of direction for herself and her career. Without the security of a record label, hundreds of thousands of fans, radio stations begging to know what the next release would be, and a bunch of songwriters pitching her their best stuff, the safety nets were gone. It was as if she were free-falling to the valley from the mountaintop with no means of slowing down. There was nothing to pick her up and make her feel good about herself and the direction she was headed. There were so few compliments left in her world.

One of her old flings, Andy Gibb, was dead. He had flamed out early, his life overdue to excessive consumption. The fast lane had eaten him alive. Within no time of his death people had even quit talking about him. It was as if his hit songs and sold-out appearances before huge crowds had meant nothing. It seemed so sad.

Tanya told *People,* "It was like Andy had everything and nothing at all." In a very real sense she could have almost been talking about herself. All the friends from her party days were gone. They had evaporated like her success and top star status. When the money ran out, they had too. If Tanya had died, would she be forgotten as quickly as Gibb? As she walked about Music City she got the idea that some folks would have preferred her in the past tense.

Tanya knew how Nashville now looked at her. It was so very obvious. In their eyes, she explained, "I was the devil." With this in mind, she should have given up, lived off the investments her father had made for her, and gone home. Yet she continued to wearily climb in the bus and hit the road. At each stop there seemed to be less glamour and fewer perks.

In the fall of 1983 Tanya performed in front of a few hundred freezing people in Forest Groves Stadium at Wake Forest University. Wake had just won a football game and most of the fans had decided to celebrate indoors where it was warm. The headliner didn't have that option. While the crowd huddled in heavy coats and blankets, she walked out in her usual stage garb. Trying to pretend it wasn't cold she cut loose with everything she had. It was a dreary day, spitting snow at times, yet she fought on even as some of the frozen crowd gave up and headed toward someplace warmer. Tanya did her best to work her body English magic on the ice-age crowd, but applause was hard to hear when those clapping were wearing gloves. She gave it all she had, and when she concluded one approving fan—one of the few who stayed for the whole set—observed, "I would have stayed to see T. if there had been twenty-five feet of snow."

At that time it would have had to snow twenty-five feet in Music City during the month of August before Tanya would get another chance at recording. Beau was trying hard, but most people simply didn't want to fool with his daughter. She probably would have faded away altogether except that the tabloid press still sought out stories that centered on Tanya. They trumpeted her drinking, her partying, her men and even her unhappiness. They hit her from every angle. Yet in a sense it was a blessing.

"My bad reputation has done wonderful things for me," she would later say. Even when the music bookers weren't thrilled by her, the tabloid press kept her in the spotlight because she was far more interesting copy than the other big acts. After all, what could you write about Barbara Mandrell?

"Me and the *National Enquirer* have been through a lot of changes over the last few years," she now told audiences. Making fun of herself and her present situation had become a way of both coping and letting her fans know that she was all right. Yet while she was laughing on the outside, on the inside she missed the old days. She also admitted that she missed the old ways the town used to work.

Tanya informed Jennifer Boeth of the *Dallas Times Herald*, "I've lost a lot of faith in record companies. They used to promote their artists. They don't do that anymore, except with a few select artists." That was Tanya's very polite way of saying that Arista and MCA had failed to support her and thus placed her in the current position in which she found herself. And in a sense it was true. With a bit of promotion they probably could have done a better job of moving her product.

She also was frustrated with the way those in Music City were turning their back on her because she didn't fit into a certain niche. Again she told Boeth, "My image constantly changes. Not like Loretta Lynn. There's an artist who knows exactly who she is. You might say she's on the mountaintop and I'm still on the road. Sometimes I feel like shouting, 'Pitch me down a rope,

Loretta!' " In this case the rope wouldn't have been long enough; Tanya was too far down the mountain.

Like any person who was struggling, Tanya was experimenting a lot. One night she would appear in jeans, another in a miniskirt. In one Jackson show her outfit, a hot-pink tank top, hot-pink earrings, hot-pink socks, hot-pink bracelet, gray shorts, and a print bandana got more press than her show.

"I change my look every day," she told those who asked. "They come to see you not hear you."

In this observation Tanya was dead wrong. Those who turned out for a Tucker concert came to hear her as much as see her. She may not have had a recording contract, but she still had one of the most recognizable voices in the business. It was that whiskey growl and can't-miss phrasing they wanted to hear. By constantly changing her look, she may have actually been confusing her fans.

After a while, she would even admit this herself. "I know that people are so confused about my image. And, if you look at all my pictures, my face changes all the time." This was Tanya's way of saying that she was confused by who she was too! And the confusion went beyond her stage show.

"I plug into the energy from an audience," she told reviewers, "and we just pitch it back and forth to each other. I thrive on adrenaline. I have to have that excitement in my life." The problem was that she was reaching for that same kind of high offstage as well.

She was partying heavy in Nashville and on the road. Sometimes she stayed out all night long. The pace she was setting for herself—the stress she was putting on her body—was taking its toll. Those around her knew it. They could sense she was in trouble. Friends and family began talking about what they were going to do.

"I'm not going to put any boundaries on it anymore," Tanya told reporters when speaking of her music. But she might as well have been talking about her life. As much as she lamented the way Andy Gibb's life had been such a waste, she didn't seem to grasp that she too was burning the candle at both ends. When those flames met, she would flame out just as quickly.

Because she wasn't on a roll, as well as her own partying, it was hard holding a band together. Musicians would get frustrated with her lack of self-discipline. They were also not a part of the new wave of country music. "Has-beens" usually have a band that is made up of loyal people and then a lot of revolving door types. Tanya had a lot of the latter. They were players who were simply using her as a rung up the ladder. Tanya was now where a lot of newcomers found themselves, a stepping-stone to use to get to the next band with nicer buses and more money. So the concerts she was doing didn't have a consistent feel. She was always breaking in someone new. Sometimes she didn't even learn their names. Other times she didn't show up for rehearsals or sound checks. A few times it was even worse.

Sometimes Tanya simply didn't show up at all. With the partying and the pain, there were days when the crowd was there and she was somewhere else. Those around her knew this was a sign of something very wrong. Tanya had always prided herself on her live show. She had once said, "I always strive to be good—to be great. When I walk offstage, if I do a bad job, my guts are ripped out. My guts are hanging in my hands. I carry them offstage with me." Now she was telling the public something far different.

"If you like someone and pay for tickets to go see his show," she explained after missing a few dates, "and he doesn't show up, sorry. That was your gamble."

You can't make a lot of money in the booking business with that attitude. The fact is that no one wants to take a chance on a star that might be two hundred miles away at a party when she is supposed to be on stage. As a result the dates Tanya was now offered were much lower end than they once had been. Still, she could write it off by simply saying it was a phase she was going through. She was just looking for herself, she would laugh.

"I haven't found my image yet," she told friends. "I think I'll probably die of trying to find it." That was what worried those around her the most.

Tanya retreated to her ranch when she wasn't on the road. "I'm taking some time off to retreat and rebuild my self-esteem," was generally what she told those who asked why she wasn't spending more time on the road. But those close to her knew that she was actually doing a great deal of cocaine and booze. "I'm addicted to anything that makes me feel good," she would later admit. With crowds not applauding as loudly, with the energy not as strong, she needed another kind of fix.

Who knows what would have happened had Tanya been picked up for possession or DWI. The press would have had a field day and her name would have been worthless in Nashville. She would have probably lost forever her ability to do the one thing that most fulfilled her—perform. Yet for the moment that didn't seem to matter to her. And every time she indulged her desires, she took another chance on ending her career.

Yet the thought of Tanya never doing another show is not what fueled her family's concern. They were frightened that she might die. They believed that she couldn't survive living the life that was now beginning to consume her. They begged her to take a look at her life and make some changes. Stubborn as always, she wouldn't listen if anyone voiced their concerns.

"It's like it says in the Ten Commandments," she jokingly would preach, "you shouldn't judge. And we all do. My God, I am a sinner too. I buy the *Enquirer*." In the midst of family and friends' concerns and worries she would often take another drink or light another cig-

arette. Then she would smile and assure them that she
was all right.

She now treated men very much the same way she
treated booze and drugs. They were only around for a
little while. Once they had been used, they were history.
She was ready to move on to another. One of Tanya's
friends told one potential suitor, "You will have a good
time, but you won't have a long time." And so it went.

More and more frustration had steered her away
from tours. In 1984 she made an appearance on "The
Love Boat" playing a rock singer who wanted a baby but
not marriage. In a sense it might have forecasted what
was waiting for her, but for now it was just an opportunity to get off the road and make some money. "I did
TV and all that stuff, but I didn't go out on the road
because I got disgusted with it," she admitted about
those days. "I was tired of it. I got tired of it because
nobody would do anything like I wanted it to be done."

When she did go on tour, she would inform her band,
"Every audience is different. Every time you walk on
stage you never know what it's going to be like." The
problem was no one knew what Tanya was going to be
like either. "People who see me today will never see me
that way again. I'll never be that way again." On some
nights people prayed that they would never have to see
anyone that way again.

She performed for a while with no set order. She
often spooked her band by simply doing whatever it was
she felt like doing. In a way she had become a geat deal
like Jerry Lee Lewis. And everyone knew that he was
really unpredictable at times.

In 1984 she worked with her brother Don on promoting the Vietnam Veterans Benefit Music Festival in
Ocala, Florida. He was now operating Don Tucker En-
terprises, a Nashville-based booking agency, and coming
off a stint as George Jones's road manager. Though he
was not a former serviceman, Don was concerned with

the plight of many men of his generation who had served in Southeast Asia. To help, he put together a benefit for the Nam Vets of Marion County and planned to use the money made to help finance a house for veterans services. Tanya, whose mind was sometimes cloudy, still had a huge heart. She answered Don's call and headlined as a favor. A few years before she might have raised a couple of hundred thousand dollars, but at this point in her career twenty-seven thousand dollars was a very nice take. The vets were pleased.

Turning often to almost rock-a-billy sound, Tanya could still light it up. She was hot and rolling when she went to San Antonio with her band and her constant road companions, a dog named Lucy and a cockatoo named Mr. T. She was in the Texas river city to work with the city's symphony. Seemingly alive with energy, she was at her sexy best, sporting an almost punk, short-haired look, complete with fishnet hose, and a minidress. She didn't look much like the finely dressed crowd, but they didn't seem to care. In the shadow of the Alamo they still loved the native Texan. Maybe, like her closing number said, this state was Heaven for Tanya. But the good times and the good crowds were not there as often as they had been in the past. In Florida she told a Cocoa writer after a show, "It's like the elephant ground out there." Things were that dead.

She would tell Diane Jennings of the *Dallas Morning News* in 1992, "I never had trouble getting work, I was just taking a few years off." But even if she didn't want to admit it, the work that was out there wasn't very appealing.

Tanya dabbled some with occasional road shows the next couple of years, but not like the frantic pace she had kept up during her heyday. More often than not the only regular place you could catch the singer was in the tabloids. She still partied, she still got crazy, and she still would occasionally appear on television, but mainly she just hung out. Finally, after a couple of years, her family stepped in to give Tanya some direction. They simply didn't want to see her waste her potential and her life. They were tired of seeing her do nothing.

"They wanted me on the road," Tanya told the press at every new stop of the tour Beau had arranged, "and I couldn't very well let everyone down." Yet it was more for her health and sense of mind than the money that her father stuck her back out on the road. And at first she really didn't want to be there.

"It is hard getting going again," she admitted a few weeks into the effort. "I haven't had a lot of hit records lately." As a matter of fact, she hadn't had any. She didn't even have a record deal. She was almost starting all over. And as the tour wore on, she began to realize that fact.

"I was off for two years," she observed. "The only thing that kept me up was I sold a lot of paper. I became a celebrity." Yet in the same breath, she admitted that she was tired of seeing her life story at the checkout stands. "I don't care for people knowing everything. I've got to have privacy in my life too."

The tabloids may have kept people curious, but a majority of the fans were still a lot more interested in Reba's music than Tanya's. Turning their attention away from the new redheaded sensation and back on herself was going to be tough. Tanya knew it. But now, for the first time in two years, as the tour wore on and she got back into stage shape, she sounded as if she were gearing up to meet the challenge.

"I want to make my family happy, I want to make the people who stayed with me through the bad stuff all happy." To do this she thought she had to climb back to the top. Yet as the record labels kept turning her away, she wondered just how she was going to do it. Maybe for the first time she was licked. This was something she didn't want to face. It was something that was never supposed to happen. She was supposed to go on forever, like Elvis.

Sadly she wondered out loud, "Maybe people don't want to hear Tanya Tucker anymore. Maybe I'm over."

- *Chapter Eleven* -

Fighting Back

Dad gets smarter as I get older.

—*Tanya Tucker*

Was Tanya all over? Had country music written her off for good?

By all rights the answer should have been yes. Logic indicated that the hurdles which she was going to have to clear to again become a major player in Music City were just too great. She was very much like the Bible's prodigal son, except in her case the father figure—Nashville's music establishment—was not waiting with open arms and offering to toss a big party. Facts were facts, she had accomplished a great deal in her early years, but there were a long list of negatives that had more recently become so much a part of her life that no one seemed ready to forget. To return to country music prominence, Tanya was going to have to fight a battle with all of her dirty linen hanging on the line for the press and public to see. So how could she do it?

First of all, the child star image which had now haunted her as it had so many others in Hollywood could never be completely forgotten, it had to be diminished. Accomplishing this objective would be like making people forget that Loretta Lynn was a coal miner's daughter, that Barbara Mandrell played a bunch of different instruments, or that Dolly Parton had a chest larger than well—larger than life. In each case the first thing people talked about when these people were discussed were these specific identifying factors. In Tanya's case the only thing that took people's minds off her rapid explosion as a child star was her fiery fifteen months spent with Glen Campbell. Being a former child star even beat being a cast-aside lover.

On top of that, country music was different now than it had been a decade before. The industry had become more like rock. It was driven by hot new groups, videos and a hit-and-run formula. The latter meant that few expected to stay around a long time, so the record labels invested as much as they could for a very short period and if the act didn't make it, then it was canceled. The old practice of letting a performer grow and build had given way to a television network mentality—if folks aren't turning in after a few weeks, then find something else. In Nashville if an act didn't have a hit by the second release, drop them and try somebody new.

This even meant that old acts had no security. They had to shoot up the charts as quickly as they had when they were leading the pack or they would find themselves without a label. MCA was about to cut Barbara Mandrell loose. Just a few years before, she had been their major female star. A car accident had interrupted her ownership of the charts and the awards. When she got back on her feet, Reba McEntire had come in and taken over. In the past a label would have kept the veteran act on board because of loyalty. Now, no matter how big a star you had once been, you were measured only on your performance at the moment.

Barbara Mandrell wasn't alone. Legends like Loretta Lynn were also on the sidelines. Like a racehorse who couldn't sprint, she had been put out to pasture. The labels weren't interested in the legend.

In this climate, how in the world could Tanya expect to get a chance to prove she could still produce? Who would even give her the time of day, much less a real chance? As had been the case for her entire career, the odds were overwhelmingly against her.

Tanya was more than aware of her tepid situation. As she observed the current climate in the industry, she marveled at hearing Patsy Cline's old recordings become hits after she had been dead for two decades. She wondered if anyone would be listening to her in two decades, much less after she was dead and gone.

Yet in reality she really didn't want to be a legend, not yet anyway. That was too easy she believed. As she told a number of friends when they were talking about Hank Williams, "You want to be a hero, all you have to do is die." She wasn't ready to die, and she certainly wasn't ready to go away, even if her name was no longer at the top of the marquee. What she wanted was something no one could conceive of—she wanted to be on top again. Her odds were probably better on her first trip to Nashville at age nine.

By 1985 Tanya was a third-billed act behind former folk rocker Michael Murphy and the unsigned and underappreciated Loretta Lynn at the Truckers Festival and Mud Bogg Competition. This was not a glamour date, and dressed in Indian leather and feathers and white boots, she met a crowd that was much more interested in trucks than Tanya. None of those in attendance figured that any of the three stars were the real deal in today's country music. But the tickets were priced right to hear a few old favorites, so they were polite and receptive. Tanya wanted more and she worked for it.

Pushing herself as she had years before, she wanted to hear cheers. She wanted to be the act that no one wanted to follow again. She was determined to make these farmers and ranchers forget Glen What's-his-name and come to their feet for "Delta Dawn." She wanted to once again be the showman who left her guts out on the stage.

"Don't confuse a good audience with a good show,"

she told her band when she finally won the crowd over. And with that she worked them harder to build a new show that was as good as any she had ever given, even back when she had them falling at her feet.

"You live for the moment when the audiences are screaming," she informed all those around her. The way she was going about her business, it seemed that she was interested in feeling that kind of high again. For the first time in several years, she was giving it her all. It was like she was trying to prove herself all over again, and she was. The first person she convinced that she was good had been Tanya Tucker. She sensed that she still could pack them in and own the spotlight. All it took was a "hell of a lot of work."

As she put more and more into each of the shows she confidently and forcefuly stated, "God put me on earth to sing, and that is what I am going to do." And with the drive and heart that seemed to exceed the size of her small frame, she literally gave it all she had. Not only were crowds responding, but the entertainers who watched her from offstage were beginning to rally around her too. Maybe she had cleaned up her act, they thought, giving her the benefit of the doubt.

Exuberant in the spotlight, offstage she was also out of her shell and very much into the world around her. No longer was she running home to hide and trying to shut the world out. She was listening, watching and finding ways to be involved again. When she heard that Bill Schroeder, the man who had been given the mechanical heart, was a big fan of hers, she didn't just write or call him, she went to see him. She brought him flowers and tapes. But unlike in the past, she didn't do it for the publicity value, she did it because she wanted him to know that she was as big a fan of his as he was of hers. She wanted him to know how much her big heart went out to him.

As they watched this new, energized version of Tanya,

those around her were beginning to smile. This was the old trooper. This was the girl who could do anything she put her mind to and never, ever, forgot a friend or a favor. This was a person on whom they could start to depend!

Still, there were things outside of her control that were constantly working against her. Most of it involved the past. In 1985 Tanya filed a $3 million lawsuit against Glen Campbell, alleging that he put her through both verbal and physical abuse when they were together. She claimed that he had fractured two of her teeth and damaged her gums and that his actions had cost her millions of dollars in bookings.

In a sense this case represented a chance for her to bury the part of her past that most haunted her. She had alluded to Campbell's alleged abuse for some time in concerts and interviews, but she had never mentioned him by name. She had always taken the high road. Now, largely because of Glen's refusing to pay the medical bills associated with the injuries he had inflicted upon her, she had gone ahead. Her lawyers had added to the bills the amount of the loss of concert dates and appearances during this time coupled with the loss of her year's bookings and her abiilty to support herself caused by Glen's desertion. The suit also noted that he did not pay her the profits from land deals in which they were both involved. In the words of the initial motion, her attorneys added, "Campbell supports the position that men such as himself may beat upon women who are smaller and weaker, but should not pick on people their own size." Still, even with the cat out of the bag, outside of court, Tanya continued to play the high ground. She didn't want to air her laundry in public, nor did she want to personally lash out against Mr. Campbell.

Tanya would eventually win an out-of-court settlement. Yet for the time being her past was once again getting in the way of the present. Who would want to pick her up with the possibility of another long line of negative supermarket gossip paper headlines? It was a question that even Tanya didn't want to answer.

In public and to the press she had an "I'm a good bet" philosophy, but out of the spotlight she had to wonder if anyone really wanted to take a risk that large. While she stated that she thought of herself as a sure thing, she had to really believe that she had a hundred-to-one shot at interesting a new label in her talents. Her rebound on stage simply couldn't translate to the recording studio, or so she was told.

Beau Tucker refused to acknowledge the odds. Just like he had over fifteen years before, he kept making the calls and knocking on the doors. He also kept telling folks, "I've got this girl who can really sing." He would have been willing to bet the farm on this, and if it had taken it he probably would have. He didn't have to play the tables, but his persistence finally paid off. He again got Tanya just what she wanted.

In late 1985 Capitol took a chance and signed Tanya up for an experimental ride. What that meant was that she had to produce in a hurry or they would show her the door. The key to keeping her on contract would probably be her old friend and producer Jerry Crutchfield. After all, he knew the singer and her talents. As the two plotted, the Capitol CEOs waited to see if the producer and artist could recapture any of the old Tucker magic.

Many around Nashville publicly asked why had Capitol taken a chance on Tucker. She was trouble, they mused. She had missed dates, had so much publicized problems with men and drug abuse and she hadn't produced a hit in years. Writers were laughing too. They were now jotting down as many notes about the crow's-feet around her eyes and her partying life-style as they were her shows and music. This new Tanya Tucker had as much of a chance as Preston Tucker had when he launched the Tucker car in 1948.

More than ever Tanya was aware that this was make it or break it time for her. She needed a hit not just for her career, but for herself personally. Those around Nashville and the press were right. Her life had not been very steady since the move to Los Angeles. She had far more downs than ups. She had no love life that offered security, her bad habits had put a strain on her once sure stage performances, and she had spent years without the drive that had once made her seem a woman in a child's body. She had to have something special in the studio or her newfound energy and direction would fade away. She prayed that Jerry could produce. Crutchfield, in a departure from the type of stuff he had once picked for her, matched her up with country's "Two Pauls."

Paul Davis and Paul Overstreet were both dynamic songwriters as well as two of Nashville's most respected people. Stable, grounded and well-liked, they seemed to come from the opposite side of the world from Tanya. Yet there was an immediate rapport between the party girl and the almost spiritual brothers of song. "One Love at a Time," penned by the two was the first thing they pitched the young woman. She liked it. It sounded very "today." The label liked it too. Now would the radio stations and the fans? "One Love" was released as a single in February. As Crutchfield and Tucker waited, Capitol began the stopwatch. If the song failed, their experiment with Tanya would probably be terminated.

"One Love" didn't let Tanya down. It charged up the charts and stayed in the numbers for an amazing twenty-five weeks. Fans demanded that stations play it. Deejays almost immediately put it into heavy rotation and kept it there for half a year. It finally peaked at #3 and country music's experts sat up and noted a potential storm warning that was being issued for another "Texas Tornado." Could she follow it up?

Jerry had no doubt because he felt that everything he and Tanya had chosen in her initial sessions had hit potential. The fact was that "Girls Like Me," released just a month after "One Love," was a great album filled with super cuts. It had been five years since Tanya had been taken seriously by the music community; they had all but forgotten that she could really get it together in the studio. Now, as they listened to the new album, it seemed that everything had been forgiven. Music City's arms were open wide. People were lining up to be the first to welcome her back. *Country Music* magazine called it, "a piece of work which far exceeds any other she had ever made in terms of depth and personal meaning."

This review and other reviewers' top-shelf words meant a great deal to the star. She had been concerned that this would just be another failure. "It's my first album in three years," she honestly stated. "My last album —no one heard it." As far as most people were concerned, it was her first really good album in almost a decade! Tanya knew that too!

Maybe that was why she worked directly with Crutchfield on all the songs for the "Girls Like Me" album. She wanted to be a part of all of it, so that if it didn't work, she could be satisfied that it had been her best. That she wouldn't have anyone else to blame.

"The songs sound like me," she explained as she listened to the initial playback. "These songs expose my heart and soul. I think it is going to be successful because it is real. I think with time I am beginning to know myself." The cover, Tanya demurely dressed and wading out of a pond, indicated that the person she had come to know was radically different from the one who posed for "TNT."

With so many gems at their disposal, Tanya and Jerry

convinced Capitol to choose "Just Another Love" for the next release. Tanya knew that this would be the song that would really decide if the public was ready to fall in love with Tanya all over again or if the last cut was simply a fluke.

Released in midsummer, Tanya celebrated her twenty-eighth birthday knowing "Just Another Love," another Paul Davis tune, was going to be her first #1 song in more than ten years. For Tanya it was a relief, but maybe not as much a relief as that felt by the folks at Capitol. They now knew that they hadn't wasted their money on a washed-up has-been. Tanya still had it.

With the hits on the board, for the first time in years the legitimate press pushed the tabloid press to one side. Tanya was now news again and they were hanging on her every word. She again didn't hold back or slip punches. She shot from the hip and gave them honest copy. Now a full-blown woman, she had decided to become a spokesperson for the women of country music.

"Nashville has long run the careers of woman singers and not allowed them a voice," Tanya explained. She even admitted that she thinks this was what had happened to her. That lack of a voice had stifled her career. She had always been too protected from career options. She assured members of the press that the men were not going to get in her way now.

Asserting her own will, she added a management team outside her family, Caribou Management. Kevin Gerard became her road manager. At that time Caribou owned CMT. The move didn't mean Beau was out of her life, she had kept him on as her personal manager, she just cut back his duties so that he could enjoy himself more. Still, when the important decisions were made, he was by her side. But the final say was now completely hers.

Tanya was looking to the future with big plans, but the

past wasn't completely buried. The public still was interested in her "good old days."

When asked about those times, Tanya told and retold the press, that her tabloid party image kept her in front of the press and public enough to prevent her career from completely dying. It may not have been a wise personal move, but it did save her career, so she was grateful that it happened. But those days are in the past, she assured fans and the media.

"I wouldn't want to live my life again. They were wild times, but they are over." But in the face of that resolve, she smoked a lot and she still drank—not as heavily as she used to, but she still was known for her ability to outdrink anyone around her. Yet now that she was making the major decisions on her career, she not only had to take more control, but she had to be more in control too. Hence a lot of the partying had to be put to one side. Tanya was relieved to get some rest.

The press now noted a more "sober" Tanya who appeared to be more sensitive and retrospective. "If I had it to do over again," she freely admitted, "there are a bunch of things I would change."

Would one of them have been Glen Campbell? She really didn't know. But showing that her sense of humor was still intact, as well as her marketing savvy, she observed what a big deal it would be if she and Glen recorded together again. It would really start everybody talking, she mused.

Love was still very much on Tanya's mind. Many wondered if she would ever love another man like she had loved Campbell. Even she wondered.

"Love should be simple," she told writer Patrick Carr, "but it's not. Hate should be hard, but it's easy."

When asked about the men in her life, she quoted a current rival. "It's like Louise Mandrell said, 'Men are attracted to me because of what I do, but when we get together then they are jealous of what I do and they don't want me to do it anymore.' What Louise said seems to be true for my life too!"

Then, after considering her situation for a while she added, "You can't break a broken heart." One would have to wonder if this statement alluded to all the pain she had experienced when she had been with Glen.

Tanya might have cut back on her drinking, but men were another situation. The once one-man woman was going through men almost as fast as she was road shows. Some were famous, some weren't, but they all liked her a lot more than she liked them. Like the legendary Mae West, she just seemed to need them around. Yet they didn't stay for long. While she would always talk in interviews about her current beau and his qualities, she would never give out his name. Her reasons were sound. "I never know how long it's going to last. By the time the press finds out who it is, I may be dating someone else."

As she approached the fall she announced, "I'm going after the young meat these days." Laughing, she turned twenty-eight on the arm of a recent college graduate. To celebrate both that milestone and her own musical comeback, she and the young bodybuilder spent a week playing in the Bahamas. A big party was held at the Tavern on the Row celebrating her birthday. She smoked one cigarette after another, bought the drinks for everyone, told the jokes and turned out the lights. Tanya may have changed a bit, but she still liked to have a good time whenever she could. She certainly wasn't in danger of having anyone mistake her for Reba McEntire or Barbara Mandrell. She hadn't become a saint, not yet anyway.

Having hits again got Tanya dreaming big dreams. She wanted management companies. She wanted to produce videos, television shows and albums. She wanted to build office buildings, truck stops and more and more and more. Just like when she was a kid, she wanted to do it all.

As her new album got hotter and hotter, as the booking dates get better and better, Tanya was almost possessed by a manic energy. She wanted to be somebody again. Deep inside her heart she was also very positive that she could find what would make her happy out there somewhere. Now, for the first time in a long time, she seemed to feel there was something great just beyond the bend, and it was almost as if she couldn't wait to get there.

With her new success, she and much of her press and fans were not looking back anymore, they were looking to the future. Tanya was beating the odds and flying in the face of conventional wisdom. This was her version of *Rocky II,* and by this time she was tired of *almost* winning. She was not going to stop clawing and scratching until the country music powers gave her one of their precious awards.

Her new single was entitled "I'll Come Back As Another Woman." She was back all right, but it appeared to be only a better version of the woman who had first thrilled Music City as a child. Of course now she was grown-up.

Chapter Twelve

Back on Top

People know that I'm no flash in the pan, that I am going to be here for the long haul.

—Tanya Tucker

/f Tanya had simply stopped producing hits in January of 1987, she would still have completed one of those miracle comebacks that are so rare in country music. In a very real sense she had been reborn. She was still the party animal, she was still "The Texas Tornado," to many she was still "The Female Elvis," and now folks were even calling her "TNT" without meaning it as a slam, but she was also a grown-up Tanya with a new perspective on how hard it was to get off the canvas and get back in the fight.

The woman who a few years before had begun to dismiss the fans as not being too important—if she decided that she wouldn't show up for a show, then that was their problem not hers—now sincerely seemed to love each and every person who came to every show and bought every tape and CD. She now would pause for pictures at a moment's notice. She would stop and sign autographs anywhere and at any time. She understood that it was these people who put the food on the table and the gas in the tank of her Mercedes. And no matter that the Mercedes sported a license plate that read "Ms. Bad Ass," it was obvious that Tanya was not nearly as bad as she would have others believe.

The reborn Tanya, the prodigal now welcomed back

to Nashville, was known to spot special people in a crowd and literally move hell and high water to get to them. She picked out Down's syndrome kids who were trying to reach for her and would push through the crowd to get to them. She made sure that someone got a picture of them with her, and then took the time to specially autograph a publicity photo of herself. Just a few years before she might not have noticed these scenes around her, now she was always on the lookout for them.

Children also got to her in the same way. If they came up to her they didn't get just an autograph, more often than not they received a hug, a kiss and a sincere, "Tanya loves you." This grown-up Tanya was fast becoming a fan favorite because the fans were her favorites. They had brought her back and reopened the doors that had been locked to her. She knew it and she appreciated it more than she could show.

In a very real sense an old bio heading had finally come true for this one-time child star. Everything was finally coming up Tanya. And there were a lot of reasons for it—good material, good production, and good promotion. But mainly it was Tanya's own enthusiasm and hunger.

As part of a lengthy interview in December 1987, Tanya told the *Nashville Tennessean*, "I am creatively on fire. I feel like a Chernobyl getting ready to go off." Those two sentences may have summed up her success much better than anything else. She was hot—not just in the marketplace, but everywhere. She was scorching the stage, the autograph lines and the recording studios. She knew what it was she wanted to be, and she had jumped on it. When Capitol had given her another chance, she had been ready to take it and run. The timing was right for both of them.

Looking back over the previous year, Tanya had reasons to feel both hot and good about life and her career.

She certainly had proven that she was no flash in the pan. She had proven she wasn't just a child star. She had proven that she was really country. And all year long she come up solid gold. Most of it was good material, but a lot of it also had to be those two hundred-plus days of road work where she was once again on top of her game. For Tanya it felt so good to be back home.

"I'll Come Back As Another Woman" was released in late '86. Most companies shy away from releasing a song just before Christmas. Many times preholiday releases are lost in the shuffle of special holiday music. Also, many people are running around getting ready for trips and parties and are not paying much attention to music and the radio. In this case, Tanya managed to hold their attention. "I'll Come Back As Another Woman" was a super follow-up to the #1 "Just Another Love." "Come Back" came home to #2.

In a very real way, the title "I'll Come Back As Another Woman" was one that signified Nashville's new acceptance of Tanya. The establishment uncharacteristically wiped her slate clean. They were now allowing her to start over and prove herself again. The switch to rock, the wild scenes in L.A. and with Glen Campbell, and the tabloid press, had been overlooked. Now only "this new woman" was the talk of the town. The past would hurt her no longer. Like a sinner at a revival, all that was expected was that she walk the line from there on in.

So for the first time in many years Tanya was now in complete control of her own fate. Her career was solidly in her hands, and she seemed ready to do all kinds of positive things with it. She was after all not simply some child star, she was a mature woman.

After "Come Back," Capitol released "It's Only Over for You" in March. While this cut only climbed as high as #8, it stuck on the charts for twenty-five weeks. The leaves were budding when it was released and falling when it faded. This song once again proved that Tanya had a following that never got tired of her music. They were charmed by almost everything she did.

In almost all of her interviews Tanya was now singing not only the praises of her new releases, but testifying to the talents of her producer. She might not have been able to find a man for her personal life, but she sure had found one for a solid professional marriage.

"I love Crutchfield," she bragged, "because he opens his heart to my mind."

Looking back, one had to wonder what would have happened if Tanya had stuck with Jerry rather than returning to the West and going the rock route. Under his guidance, she might have moved to the top of the country female singers before she was twenty. She might have even approached Loretta Lynn legend status before she turned thirty. Would she have cut off the rise of Barbara Mandrell or Reba McEntire? We will never know, but it was something to ponder, and don't think that Beau Tucker, Tanya and Jerry didn't think about it too. If only . . .

Besides the wonderful material which was being churned out by Capitol, besides the new rave reviews for her road shows, Tanya had made solid use of a new hot medium sweeping country music. She was great on camera. Between videos and live shots on "Nashville Now" and other TNN talk shows, she won points with viewers every time they turned the TV on. She was natural, cute, funny, and over the tube she could even evoke special feelings that seemed to reach and touch people's heart. She also had sex appeal.

"I think sexiness comes from within," she said when asked why she was viewed as being so very hot. "A woman is either sexy or she's not."

Evidently Tanya was. When surfing through cable selections, if Tanya popped up on the screens, people often stopped. She was a "zapper stopper." This put her in league with people like Vanna White and Jane Seymour, and the television executives loved people who could manage to focus attention on their own images. They were so easy to sell. This was working to advantage, and it would become even more important as the medium expanded.

With songwriters Paul Davis and Paul Overstreet giving Crutchfield a batch of their creative genius on a regular basis, Tanya's midsummer release of the album "Love Me Like You Used To" cemented her return to country music superstardom. The title single hit #2 of Billboard's charts. The cut was another one with a very long shelf life. "Love Me" hung around in major rotation for twenty-five weeks.

In late November, a single where Tanya was vocally backed by the songwriting duo of Davis and Overstreet spent twenty-four weeks on the charts. "I Won't Take Less Than Your Love" would become Tanya's eighth #1 record.

It was strange that Paul Davis was included on the particular cut. Although responsible for much of Tanya's great material, Davis was not the writer of this song. "I Won't Take Less Than Your Love" had been composed by Overstreet and Don Schlitz. Those two had woven magic for Randy Travis with "Forever and Ever, Amen," and they would strike gold many more times for many more artists. This time it was Tanya who would put the change in their pockets. Yet it was Davis, rather than Schlitz, who was invited to sing along because he was a solid vocalist and Tanya considered him an important part of her new team.

Tanya's admiration for the songwriters was not a solitary one. All around Nashville people were now giving the two Pauls a great deal of the credit for Tanya's new success. They deserved it. They seemed to understand not only Tanya's vocal strength, but how to write in ways which she could stylize and sell. People who listened to her shape and sing the two Pauls' lyrics, actually believed that she meant them. There seemed to be a spiritual connection among the three of them that transmitted so well to her records. Yet there was more too.

Paul Overstreet's friendship was beginning to prove an important facet of Tanya's personal life too. She knew that he had been through some rock-bottom times before he had turned himself around. She knew that he had searched for happiness in a bottle but only found it through his Christian faith and the peace it brought. She also found that he was more than happy to share with her where he had been, how low he had sunk, and just how happy he was now. She began to really enjoy talking to Paul because he was as real as she was, and he was so happy too. A wonderful spouse, a solid marriage, great kids and a feeling for just what he wanted to do and be in life, made him a person who she could look to and learn from. Best of all, he never preached. He was there when she needed him, but he never looked down on her. He understood, he didn't judge.

Tanya may have been listening and thinking about Overstreet's "devil in the bottle" stories, but she wasn't ready to apply them to her own life. Her life was still filled with great passions. She had a passion for wine, men and song. She loved to dance. She loved great food. She loved living her success to its fullest. She enjoyed stepping over the line.

"I really enjoy being free and fun and taking it beyond the limits sometimes," she informed the press at almost every tour stop. And she tried to live up to her words. But it wasn't as easy as it once had been. Too often the old crowd wasn't there to join her. She was dismayed that many of her past party friends now wanted to spend time at home. They had families and real jobs. They couldn't party to dawn and go to work the next day. They couldn't find a baby-sitter on the spur of the moment. They couldn't drop their lives for her now. She understood, but it made her feel even more lonely.

The hurt also came when she realized that she had shared a secret about something very personal with a long-time friend and then they had passed it on. It happened to her a great deal, and she should have quit trusting her friends, but she didn't. She continued to tell them matters of the heart and they didn't always respect the private nature of these stories. Sometimes this secret news—the stories of parties and men—hit the tabloid press almost before the phone lines were cold.

"I am trying to laugh at myself," she said about the stories, "I am trying to laugh at everything." But she cried because she couldn't believe that people would use her trust just to get a few bucks. The hotter she got, the more she realized that she could only trust a rare few people.

Tanya was no longer working small shows. She was back in the big time working the top houses. She began 1988 appearing on the road with Hank Williams, Jr. and opening for the Oak Ridge Boys. Now the crowds were coming out for her as much as they were for the men. Because her show was so tight, because her songs were so hot, and because her performance was so electric, other stars once again dreaded following her. Just like the old days, once Tanya left the stage, the crowd didn't have any energy left. She had delivered the knockout punch, and now the final act must play to a crowd that was lying on the canvas.

In many ways this new Tanya did appear to be the same one who wowed them as a teen. Yet the lines on her face, the years of being out of the spotlight, as well as the life she had led, had dramatically altered the real woman. When asked how much she had changed since she had her first hit record, she would sigh, "I still sign my name the same." She knew that the innocent little girl was long gone, and so were the innocent days that rode with that child.

Between the partying and touring, as well as all the hard work, Tanya was beginning to get tired and worn down. By early '88 it showed in her eyes, if not in her attitude. "I won't kick back until I accomplish what I want to accomplish," she vowed. But those around had other ideas.

Friends like Mae Axton, a songwriter who had penned Elvis's first gold record, "Heartbreak Hotel," thought Tanya was out of control and needed some help. Like so many others, Mae believed that the partying was going to either kill her or her career. "She needed some education before things got worse," the songwriter pointed out.

While her family and close friends worried, Tanya remained in a state of denial. She didn't think she needed to quit anything, and she wanted to get the preaching people off her back. But they wouldn't stop, so the questions kept coming.

When she was asked if she had ever had any real trouble with her life-style, the real story began to come out in what Tanya didn't say. "At least I've had fun. I'm proud of it, and I'm not going to deny it anymore. I'm trying to quit smoking. I'm trying to quit doing a lot of things." But she wasn't quitting anything very quickly.

As the first month of the year closed out, this "I'm addicted to anything that makes me feel good" attitude had gone on as long as Beau and Juanita could take it. They were concerned that their little girl was going to kill herself with her life-style. They wanted her to get help. To make the point they canceled her tour and confronted her at home. What they again realized was that Tanya didn't want to face the facts they were laying out. She wouldn't admit that she needed any kind of help. This time that didn't stop her family. She may have kicked and she may have screamed, but she was put on a plane headed west. Beginning on February 2, 1988, her address was the Betty Ford Clinic.

Tanya was still not convinced she had any real problems. Even while undergoing treatment, she lashed out. She often refused to participate in group sessions. She wouldn't admit past problems. A lot of times she wouldn't talk. She vented her anger in her journals, and she felt she had good reasons to be mad. She was angry that a star on the rise could be treated as a common drunk. She was angry that her folks had turned on her. She was angry that she was a prisoner. And she was just angry because she was angry. She counted the days until she got out and told those who visited with her, "There are all kinds of people in here in a lot worse shape than I am."

When finally pressed to take a look at what cocaine was costing her, Tanya shrugged and stated that the drug problem was mainly boredom. It was something to do when things were slow on the road or at home. It livened things up. But it wasn't something she needed, and she could give it up if she had to.

A worried LaCosta told *People,* "I just want Tanya to be happy. That has always been hard for her." And the Betty Ford Clinic certainly didn't seem to bring the star any closer to real happiness.

Upon getting out Tanya told Nora Villagran of the *Mercury News,* "I did six weeks hard time. They tried analyzing me, looking inside to find out what was wrong with me. They couldn't accept the fact that I just like to party and have a good time."

Nevertheless, while smoking a cigarette and sipping on a beer, she informed the press she had quit the all-night bar-hopping. She was going to keep an eye on things so that people won't bother her about her lifestyle. She didn't want to be preached at anymore. And she certainly didn't want to go back to that place!

Tanya's six weeks away from the business didn't hurt her at all in the marketplace. "It Don't Come Easy," which could have been the story of Tanya's current troubles, was the final single off the "Love Me Like You Used To" album. Released in April 1988, it hung on the charts for five months and hit the top spot just before Independence Day.

"You know I didn't like that song at first," Tanya remembered. "After I cut it I liked the words and it grew on me. I've had a lot of people, especially women, who told me the song gave them strength." The David Gibson/Craig Karp cut would be the singer's ninth #1.

Tanya's last two albums, the first Capitol releases, both pushed three hundred thousand units each. This was outstanding for that time in country music. With these numbers Tanya has sold eight million records total during her career. Yet none of the huge numbers seemed to satisfy her. She wanted more. She wanted to sell like the top male acts did.

At this point only the Judds and Reba were approaching those numbers. And both of those acts were still well behind their male counterparts. The reason was simple; women bought most of the country music albums and while women may like to listen to women on radio, they spend their money on men in the stores. Tanya wanted to change that, and with the kind of records she was now cutting, she sensed that she could.

Something else was driving Tanya too. It was an internal clock that was ticking louder with each passing year. She was beginning to feel her maternal instincts pushing out, and she knew that she had not even come close to finding a man whom she could trust and love as a husband. As always, the fact that she wasn't in the right place or the right time didn't keep Tanya from talking about her dreams.

"You know," she mused, "I'd probably make a great

mother." If the "reformed" party girl then saw an eye-brow raise, she would add, "So many times people you think would make the worst moms make the best ones." Then she would laugh. At that point everyone would think, what a joker. Who could picture Tanya with a baby?

There were other times when her voice grew more sad as she admitted, "I put off having kids, and now I don't know if I will ever have any."

She then told writer Jack Hurst, "I certainly ain't interested in getting married; I may have kids, but I don't think I'm interested in marrying nobody." At that time no one took her seriously. Yet as always, when Tanya talked about something, she usually had a plan in the back of her mind that she was ready to implement.

Sensing her daughter's loneliness and considering her past and recent personal problems, Juanita Tucker told *People*, "I just wish Tanya would get married and have a little girl. That's all she needs." Yet while there were a lot of guys lining up, none of them, even the ones who were classified as gentlemen, seemed to hold the singer's attention for very long. They were just toys, something to play with and then throw away.

When "Love Me Like You Used To" became her first Billboard top ten LP since "TNT," Tanya was seen with a bear. At that point the new man in her life was Chicago Bears offensive lineman Tom Thayer. Everyone around thought he was a great guy. Maybe just the kind who could tame the Tornado and sweep her off her feet. Still she was touring too much to see him very often. And like all of the others, he would just fade away.

Of marriage she told Bruce Honick of *Nashville Scene*, "I don't know if that day is ever gonna come. I have to have someone that's really an understanding soul that will hold his own and is not intimidated by the fact that I have a lot of fans, and that kind of thing, and people are going to be interrupting my meals and asking for my autograph, which is fine."

A few nights later she told a concert crowd, "Toss me a rich old millionaire with a bad cough."

Then, in the middle of a series of concert gigs Tanya tiredly exclaimed, "I'm glad I don't have kids, I'm glad I'm not married! That would tie me down too much!"

She was certainly busy. Except for her time at Betty Ford she was always on the move. When not in the recording studio, on television, doing videos, racing from concert to concert and interview to interview, she found other ways to occupy herself.

She put together a Celebrity Downhill Ski Tournament in Steamboat Springs. The competitive edge came out as she raised money for charity while making others eat her snow flakes.

She also got back into the animal scene by naming and following one of the eagles that was being rereleased in the state of Tennessee. These bald eagles had come from Alaska and were part of a nationwide program to repopulate the continental United States with our native symbol. Tanya eagerly volunteered to be a part of that. She had to be a sponsor. After all, if the bald eagle did make a comeback, it probably wouldn't be any greater than the one she was making at that moment. So they had a great deal in common.

Still she told David Zimmerman of *USA Today* in October 1988, "I've always disliked the word *comeback.*" Tanya preferred to think of herself as having been away but having still maintained her status. In all honesty, this simply wasn't the case. She had come back further than anyone in recent times in country music. If there had been a CMA award for comeback kids, she would have won it going away.

And recognition was finally coming her way too. At the time when the "Strong Enough to Bend" album and single were released the Country Music Association nominated her for Best Female Vocalist. It was her first nomination since she was fifteen—a half a lifetime ago. In a very real way, "Strong Enough to Bend," written by Don Schiltz and Beth Nielson-Chapman, signaled a final step to having Music City welcome her back. For Tanya it was more than a song, it was a moment to remember and treasure. She was back at the top. She was flying with eagles. What more could she want now?

On October 22, "Strong Enough to Bend" hit the top of the charts. It came just a little more than a week after the CMA had overlooked Tanya for their top female award. No matter, she knew that things were going to continue to come her way. And in this case she really was strong enough to bend and to wait for the awards. At thirty she was getting itchy about other things.

Earlier in the year Tanya had asked Beau if he would mind if she had a baby without benefit of marriage. His rather strong reaction indicated that he was against it in a big way. It was not only the wrong way to have a child, he thought, it would also wreck her career. She thought about his words but considered her own needs and desires even more. She would not be denied. As the days passed she was simply marking time. She was also making a real effort to change her life-style in preparation for her next goal.

"I'm a different person now," Tanya explained to friends and press as she cut back on her partying. On her two thousand-acre ranch she thought about her life. In the old days she would have been surrounded by friends and entertaining a good-looking man, now she was often alone. Her bedroom door had a sign overhead that said, NO ONE GETS TO SEE THE WIZARD. NOT NO ONE. NOT NO ONE." At least not until she found the right one, and she was praying that this day would be soon.

In late 1988 "Highway Robbery" was released and lingered on the charts for nineteen weeks, falling just short of #1. Still few women would complain about having the second place song on the charts, and Tanya certainly wasn't going to do much more than smile. She was back and what could stop her now?

- Chapter Thirteen -

A Baby

I want to tour and record as long as I can breathe.
—Tanya Tucker

As time began to separate Tanya from her days in the Betty Ford Clinic, she began to speak out more often on the effect of drugs on her life. What she said had to be comforting for the staff at Ford, for her family, the Nashville establishment and her fans. "It [drug use] is just a road to nowhere, and once you realize that, you lose your taste for those sort of things."

Ever honest, she seemed to be no longer in denial. Still she wouldn't lie and tell people that the times she had were a complete waste. But she now had placed enough distance between herself and those times to at least be able to put things into perspective.

"I had a lot of fun," she honestly admitted. "I met a lot of crazy, wild people. I mean some strange people do drugs, you know. They're fun to be with and that kind of thing. The actual doing it and being around it, that was fun. The afterwards was always the hard part. There's a certain amount of loneliness too, especially for a person my age. I'd come home after working and there I'd be alone. That is when the addiction starts."

Admitting she once had a problem probably moved her up Music City's ladder of respect a few notches. In a very real sense she seemed like she was continuing to reform. While no one expected her to embrace religion like a Connie Smith, many did expect her to become a woman who—while still having a glint of mischief in her eye—would carry herself more like a Reba or a Dolly.

One of these was her record label. Capitol, a company once laughed at for signing Tanya, now wore a big smile every time her name was mentioned. They had a huge star on the payroll and now that the star had cleaned up her drug problem there seemed to be nothing ahead that could keep her off the charts. Their gamble had paid off in a big way.

"I want to be remembered as one of the world's greatest entertainers," Tanya openly stated once again. This statement, the confidence that went with it, the focus that was apparent every time she said it, made her sound much like the teen Tanya. She seemed ready to conquer the world and become a part of country music history.

This new, conservative and almost predictable Tanya, the woman who had confronted her past and regained her status as a top country music act, could now be covered and publicized just like any other female superstar. She had become a part of the establishment. There didn't have to be a disaster relief team following her around. There were no real worries that accompanied her on tour. At the rate she was going the tabloids would soon be tired of assigning reporters to follow her.

Yet what the press didn't know and what for that matter her label and her family didn't realize was that Tanya had something revolutionary on her mind. What she had planned would make her move to rock a few years before look like a walk in the park.

As she approached her monumental thirtieth birthday, Tanya decided that she wanted a baby and she decided to have one come hell or high water. She had talked about a child and motherhood a great deal with friends and family over the preceding months. Yet few took her seriously. They thought she was just wishing or dreaming. And if she was going to make a move, most would have assumed that she would have adopted an orphan. That was the generally accepted and honored route for a single woman to become a mother.

The latter approach would have probably canonized her and lifted her to Barbara Mandrell status in Nashville. If Tanya had taken it upon herself to open her arms and home to a starving, hungry, deserted child, as Roy Rogers and Dale Evans had done so many times, it would have been big news everywhere. The newsmagazines would have jumped on it, television would have been there, ministers would have even been talking about Tanya's loving heart during sermons. It probably would have brought her enough goodwill to earn her a suitcase full of awards. Yet, that was not the road she chose to take.

She later explained to the famous sexologist, Dr. Ruth, how she went about making good on her very personal decision. "I wanted a child and on my thirtieth birthday I decided that I'd have a baby. It just happened that I had a relationship with this person which didn't work out. We discussed it in depth; he knew it was what I wanted. It wasn't the only thing I wanted out of the relationship—I would have loved to have made it work —but it wasn't right."

The man who would become the father of Tanya's child was a former college athlete. The two met at a 1988 Tulsa concert. Tanya was immediately attracted to him, so much so that she hired him to do a guest shot in a video that she was about to shoot.

On the set of *Strong Enough to Bend,* she and Ben Reed continued the physical chemistry that had been evident upon their first meeting. While they didn't become a part of the tabloid gossip pages, they saw each other and visited enough to continue to have a somewhat steady relationship.

Reed had cover boy good looks. The overused phrase,

tall, dark and handsome fit him to a tee. Tanya would have loved to have labeled him her "Sir Galahad." Yet while his looks were right, she couldn't develop that forever and ever love she needed to stop her search for her ideal man. Still he was a step above most men she dated. She had a genuine affection for him.

As she approached her birthday she found herself in need of not only someone to share the "thirtieth" with her, but also to escort her to the Country Music Association awards show at the Opry House. As always the award show would be broadcast on the CBS television network, and with country music so hot, the ratings promised to shoot through the roof. With Tanya nominated for the big female award, she knew that the cameras would cast their eyes on her several times in the audience. Hence she wanted the man beside her to stand out. She called Ben and he came to spend the day and night with her.

The two of them attended the CMA awards together on October 10. Tanya looked fabulous, as did her date, but it was Kathy Mattea who took the title of Female Vocalist of the Year. Coming up empty was not the kind of birthay present for which Tanya had hoped.

After post awards birthday wishes from all, she and Reed retired to spend the night together. He was looking forward to a wonderful evening with a woman he admired and liked a great deal. She thought the timing was right for something much more. It was that night that Tanya got her wish and a child was conceived.

Ideally, in a proper storybook form, Tanya and Ben should have fallen in love and gotten hitched the very next day. It would have made such a wonderful story. But what actually happened was that the two fought. Disgusted with him, Tanya put him on a plane back to Tulsa. She wouldn't see him or call him for nine months. In a very real sense, his purpose served, he had been booted off the team.

By Thanksgiving Tanya knew she was pregnant. Never one to hold back news from her family, she told them that she was expecting a child. She related the whole story. To say the least, Beau and Juanita were disappointed. Telling her parents and having them decide how they were going to handle this issue was one thing, but what about the record label and the bookers? What were they going to say? A meeting had to be called.

Tanya walked into that meeting, single, pregnant and proud. She announced that she had no plans to get married, that she wasn't in love with the father, and on top of that she was not going to name him in the press.

"I don't care what people say," she told them.

The record company and management team then asked her how they were supposed to handle this? They felt she had to identify the twenty-three-year-old ex-West Virginia quarterback as the father. If she didn't, along with some moral apology, they feared that the Bible Belt would crucify their best-selling female artist. They believed that millions of fans would burn her records and tapes in protest.

Tanya was defiant. "I'm not going to say a damn word, it is nobody's business but mine."

But what about the career?

Tanya tried to tell them that the career would survive. She had made it through worse things than this she explained. Who was going to hate her for having a child? After all, Goldie Hawn had done it. So had a host of other Hollywood types, and their careers were going fine. In the long run, she assured them, this was not going to be a big deal.

As the meeting broke up and the days dragged on, everyone beside Tanya was convinced that she had written off any chances at continuing to be a force in country music. They could imagine fans staying away in droves and deejays refusing to put her on the playlist. It was almost as if a black cloud had settled over the Capitol headquarters.

Once the news hit the streets, Tanya didn't try to hide the fact that she was going to have a baby. As a matter of fact, she acted like she was real proud of that fact. Jumping on her, the tabloids trashed her again. They had been hungry for something good, and now they had it. They bounced around all kinds of names for the prospective father. Yet Tanya still wouldn't talk. She actually didn't care.

Being pregnant was bad enough in Nashville, but the fact that she was so "damn" proud of having done it started people talking and kept them talking. Outrage seemed to be the emotion that best fit the establishment which Tanya had just become a part of. Now she was once again out of the club.

Ironically it may have just been the act of getting pregnant that led to Tanya finally leaving the immaturity of childhood behind. Up until this time she had no reason to grow up. She had a loud voice in, but didn't really run her business. As long as she made money she could party like a teenager and there were no real repercussions except in the tabloids. In her private life she really could do whatever she wanted and it made no difference. Now things were changing. She was going to have to really look at herself, her life and what she represented. She was going to have to grow up and take charge of her affairs. She was also going to have to take better care of herself so that she would be assured of having a healthy child. This process would be one that would prove as unsure and unsteady as the career that had consumed almost all of her previous years. Yet it was one that had its beginning in the creation of this child.

Initially, in spite of the bad press, concert attendance was not hurt too badly by her condition. Of course now she could not work as much or push as hard. And certainly as she became more and more obviously pregnant, her Elvis-like moves had to be cut back. But considering how bad things could have been, she seemed to be surviving just fine. Her shows were making money, and no one was burning her records. So far things were reasonably fine.

Then in May of 1989 Tanya was called to court. On the stand she had to admit that she had used cocaine in 1987. The woman she had used it with two years before had been charged with murder. If Capitol had been upset before, now they were really gnashing their teeth. Just when they thought that the scandals were all behind their star, they had two very public ones going down at once. Unapologetic, Tanya still let it slide. She admitted her drug use, gave her testimony and walked out. She was expecting and happy, and that was all that mattered to her. What people said didn't seem to matter a bit to her.

"Why get married," she told the press on several occasions. "Hearts change and when they do the money goes with them." Words like this didn't usually play too well in the Bible Belt. Those around Tanya couldn't believe that she was saying them.

With some trepidation, Capitol released "Call On Me" at the same time Tanya had been put on the stand in the courtroom. It wouldn't have surprised them to see the single die on the vine. Instead it hung around for nineteen weeks and didn't stop climbing until it made #4. "Call On Me" also helped continue the surge in sales of the "Strong Enough to Bend" album. The record executives breathed a little easier as the song climbed. Still they wondered if their luck could hold once the baby was actually born and the news media really jumped on Tanya. What they needed was some good news—some good publicity on which they could hang their hats and hopes.

Tanya's close friends, who grew fewer as the due date

grew closer, tossed her a baby shower on June 11. After they finished passing out gifts, they went to supper. During the meal fate gave Tanya a chance to do something very positive. Sitting across from the expectant mother, Rosemarie Farone began to choke on a piece of food. Racing to her, Tanya performed the Heimlich maneuver and saved the woman from choking to death. The story made almost every paper in the United States. It was just the kind of thing Capitol would have set up if they had thought of it. In the midst of the storm, they had seen a patch of blue sky. Tanya didn't put much stock in this good press. As a matter of fact, the press and what they wrote didn't seem to bother her at all. She had too many other things on her mind.

Besides her own child, Tanya had another baby she was working on. She was putting together a new video as a present and tribute for her father. One of his favorite singers had been the legendary Jimmy Rodgers. Tanya had recorded Rodgers' "Daddy and Home" and matched it with a video which showed Beau and photos from his life. The song was scheduled to be a part of her "Greatest Hits" album to be released in July. She was more excited by this song and video than she was the album.

"Daddy, I'm coming home, your little girl is coming home to you," the words cried out. Tanya cried as she picked out the photos for the video. Each shot moved her to want to reach out to her own father. She was so caught up in the project that she even took an active role at Nashville's Scene Three production facilities. She wanted her fingerprint on every part of this "father's day" card. "Daddy and Home" was released in mid-July. While it didn't set the charts on fire, only topping out at #27, Tanya had made a very public statement to the most important man in her life. It was something she wanted to accomplish before she awarded him his newest grandchild.

The event which had caused Nashville's tongues to wag for more than half a year finally came to pass on July 5. That particular Wednesday was not one of woe for Tanya. After a tough Cesarean delivery the star looked at her seven-pound, six-ounce baby girl and announced, "I have done it all now!" Around the nation there would be many that would have wholeheartedly agreed with her statement. She had done just about everything, except get married.

Tanya chose the name Presley Tanita for her new little girl. The child was named after Elvis and her mother. She admitted that it was "not your average name for a baby, but she is not your average baby." Certainly no one would have argued with that. There was no way that one of Tanya Tucker's children could be average.

The hospital room at Vanderbilt Medical Center looked like a florist shop. Tanya actually had flowers given to other patients just to make room for visitors. Tired, she was glowing. Yet some questioned why she hadn't invited the child's father for the birth. She had her reasons and she shared them in 1992 with Diane Jennings of the *Dallas Morning News*. "I didn't want the father present for my child's birth because giving birth is very personal." To Tanya the birth was far too personal to invite a man she didn't love to share. In Tanya's eyes it was her moment. She had planned it, she had conceived how to accomplish it, and she had carried the unborn babe alone for nine months.

At that time no one outside of those closest to her family and business operations knew that Ben Reed was the father. In the press she even claimed that she had not contacted him to tell him he was the one. "But he's no fool," she would point out. "He can count, he knows."

When reporters tried to point out that excluding the father was not something generally done even in these circumstances, Tanya shot back, "I've never done any-

thing the normal way, this is just one more example."
The fact was, that for the child's first half year, Reed
was totally removed from Presley's life.

Right after the child's birth Tanya, accompanied by
LaCosta, spent a week at a California spa getting rid of
the baby fat. "I want to be the hard body of country
music," Tanya informed the press. Considering she had
just given birth, she quickly got back in great shape.

"I'd like to take a year and just be with my baby," she
admitted. But because of this move, many believed that
her career was in danger of falling apart. With the future in mind, her child's future that is, in August, Tanya
was ready to hit the road. With the child in tow she
jumped back on stage and got to work. But for the first
time in a long time, her career wasn't the primary driver
in her life. "I now have something more important in
my life than my music."

The road is a rough life-style for a child, any child,
and Tanya would lose a great deal of sleep playing both
mamma and star. She would also catch a great deal of
criticism for taking the child on the bus with her. And
that really wasn't fair. Barbara Mandrell had usually
been praised for taking her children with her. Others
had been all but canonized for being road mothers, but
not Tanya. In spite of the fact that she had redone her
bus, brought along her mother and hired a nanny, folks
seemed to take pleasure in pointing out that she was
bringing up this illegitimate child in a horrible manner.
In all honesty it wasn't the bus and hotels that were
bothering most of them, it was the fact that she wasn't
married.

Moral thinking getting in the way of real facts would
continue to hurt Tanya in the press and with some of her
fans. Many were not willing to leave her alone. They
may have been able to overlook the long parade of affairs and drug use and still stay turned on to her as a
performer, but they couldn't forget her "immorality"

when they saw a child in her arms. In their eyes the baby was living proof of just what kind of woman Tanya really was.

While Beau and Juanita had been hurt by the way this had all happened, they had reached out to Presley with the same love they had for Don and LaCosta's children. The grandparents quickly gave Presley their undivided attention. They were bound and determined to do the best job they could at spoiling her. And as Tanya became the subject of more sermons and editorials, they rallied to her side as only parents could.

As she held her child, Tanya often marveled at having made it to thirty, much less made it to motherhood. By all rights she knew that she could have very easily been dead. Her life-style should have killed her. Yet even though she breast-fed Presley for more than half a year, and during much of this time she ate carefully and watched her drinking, she still had some rough edges. And she didn't shy away from talking about them.

While she still liked to party, Tanya admitted that even when she went out she didn't enjoy herself much because she was always thinking about her daughter. Many times she canceled her plans just to spend time with Presley. She also tried to be more careful about the kind of people she brought home. She wanted only good influences around her daughter. That fact in itself seemed to close the door on some of the wilder party crowd that was a part of her past. She had also cut back on her drinking, and smoking was her only visible and dramatic vice.

Tanya placed her mind in a forward mode and again considered the rain forest, the fate of whales and harp seals. She thought and spoke about the world that might not be there for her daughter in the future. She wanted to do something to stop pollution. She was looking ahead at a bigger legacy than just music. Once again she was opening her heart in special ways.

When she saw hungry children in the third world on television she had to turn it off. Because of her daughter she couldn't disassociate herself from the pain of other children. Those around Tanya started to realize that the child was really forcing the mother to take a second look at life—to grow up.

Trying to think of a life beyond show business Tanya started Tanya Tucker Jeanswear, Inc. and added a P.T. line for toddlers. The denim clothes were produced in factories in Alabama and Tennessee. Rather than help her future, the line quickly died. Part of the failure was blamed on her marital status. Still she kept moving forward, not looking back.

Tanya discovered that her concert crowds were now often made up of single women with children. They were looking to her as a role model. Never before had she considered herself a role model for anyone. It was a very sobering thought. "Single mothers walk up to me all the time and tell me they are with me. I'm a role model for those women who have always been alone with no support." This was a responsibility which Tanya could get into. If given a chance, she would turn this cause into an organized effort.

When the vice president Dan Quayle lashed out at a television character for having a child out of wedlock, Tanya saw her chance and jumped into the fray. For years she had been forced to listen as people preached at her, now it was her turn to take to the pulpit. She did so loudly. Standing up proudly, she informed the world that there were an awful lot of great single parents out there and the Veep didn't know what he was talking about. She kept preaching at every stop she made on her concert tour.

She told *Country Music*'s Patrick Carr, "Things have changed. There's a lot of single mothers out there, women who can't find true love, or . . . well, look at the divorce rate and the abortion issue. I couldn't help but win on this subject, you know? Who's going to tell me I should have an abortion, or get married to someone I know I'm not in love with?"

In some ways having Presley was a great publicity stunt. It was Glen Campbell without the pain and anguish. It was news that allowed her to present something positive to her public. She could say, *Yeah, you may disagree with the method, but how can you call this beautiful child a mistake?* To really make this concept work, wherever she went, she took the child proudly with her. On "Crook and Chase," "Nashville Now," "Video PM," "Entertainment Tonight," and even in print interview sessions, she held the baby and put people in a position of having to say good things. She made it all but impossible for anyone to publicly criticize her. Once again she was using the press, getting in the press, and becoming even a bigger story than her latest release or video. Tanya was news, and she knew the value of being news. She knew that people were lining up to interview her, and she didn't disappoint them.

"In a sense I really feel like I have come home," she said about motherhood. On the outside it really did seem to have glued together a new bond in the Tucker family. It made the old ones more significant too. She and her father didn't quarrel as much anymore and she didn't seem to have the rebel edge she once had. As the weeks rolled by, she appeared to be slowing down more and enjoying the simple things in life.

She told Marjie McGraw of *Country Song Roundup,* "When you get real stressed out and you think, 'I want to go get drunk. I want to go and see some of my old friends—just party and write songs,' but my baby keeps me stabilized. Being a mother is an incredible responsibility. I thank God for her every day, because she's an amazing piece of artwork. To think that she came from me is pretty mind-boggling."

"Presley was God's way of letting me know that I

have to let go of it [wild life-style]," she told Valerie
Hansen of *Country Spirit* in 1994 when asked to look
back at her party days. Then she smiled and added, "I
hope that Elvis would have been happy with this name.
It's just too bad it couldn't have been some of his sperm
also." In a sense she was a different, more stable Tanya,
but in another, she hadn't changed all that much. She
still liked to shock people. One gets the idea that Mae
West would have loved Tanya Tucker. They were very
much cut from a similar mold.

In October 1989, Tanya celebrated her thirty-first
birthday at Opryland's Magnolia Room with a live band
and four hundred guests. For what may have been a
first, the party was dry and no one was allowed to
smoke. Guests included Robin Lee, Freddy Weller,
Garth Brooks, the Nitty Gritty Dirt Band, Jeanie Seeley,
Paulette Carlson and Marie Osmond. Outfitted to the
nines in a low-cut, floor-length black dress and elbow-
length white gloves, the star's hair was pulled back
tightly against her head. She looked anything but the
part of a wild woman. Under it all she wore red cowboy
boots. She appeared to be a Texas princess, a member of
the American royal family. But the look didn't mean she
was blessed with good fortune.

A few days later, once again nominated at the CMA
awards, she was again beaten. Yet this time it didn't
seem to matter as much. In her daughter she had the
one award she had really always wanted—at least in her
adult years.

On the lack of award recognition she lamented after
the show, "I was disappointed. I think anybody would be
a fool to say they weren't. I thought I had it this year. I
thought I had it last year too. I had so many hit records
out that year. Maybe they are tired of seeing my name
up there."

That could have been the case, or maybe it was the
past history or the new child without benefit of mar-

riage. The year had seen her "Greatest Hits" LP climb charts in a hurry. It had also seen "Highway Robbery" and "Call On Me" become hits, but it wasn't as strong a year as 1988. And Presley and the talk around the birth had been much bigger news than her career. So, maybe Kathy Mattea was the right choice after all.

Shrugging her shoulders, Tanya added, "I've sort of given up on it. The best award I have is when I look out at the audience and the seating is full."

She now had the child too, and that had put a building career on hold. Could she push it up a notch and reclaim the momentum she had possessed in 1988? Many were wondering, but few were betting on Tanya now.

- Chapter Fourteen -

Riding the New Wave

*Country has changed. There is now a huge
audience for it.*

—Tanya Tucker

It seemed hard to believe that Tanya Tucker was now
getting into her fourth decade in the entertainment
business. But it was here—the nineties. She had begun
work in the sixties, hit the top in the seventies, fallen
hard and begun the climb back up in the eighties, and
now, with a new child in tow, was trying to reshape the
limits and thinking of those who loved country music in
this decade. Her newest challenge might very well have
been her toughest.

Her first single in the "new mother era" was "My
Arms Stay Open All Night." The folks at Capitol were
still waiting to see if the bottom would drop out of her
sales. They were still expecting a fallout from the moral
majority. Yet there didn't seem to be one.

Booking demand by huge arenas was up. Radio
playlists were not backing away from the unwed mother.
Even when she announced the father's name and that
she had no interest in marrying him, it didn't seem to
cause people to back away from her. People may have
been a little shocked that Tanya would do such a thing
as have a child without a husband, but they had been
shocked the first time they saw her bump and grind on
stage when she was thirteen. Tanya had been shocking

them for close to two decades. They were used to being shocked.

The William Morris Agency was much more interested in her show than they were her child. They had booked her since she slipped into rock, but they had never really paid much attention to what she looked like —how she was presented. Now they determined that they needed to put some money into her costuming, staging and lighting. They wanted her to look as classy as Reba. They also wanted her to win a few awards so that they could make even more money from her two hundred shows a year. So the booking agency dressed up the band and show, made it classier, and booked her in larger arenas. She also was no longer opening for other acts. She was now headlining over hot new performers such as Billy Dean, Aaron Tippin, Mark Collie and Brooks & Dunn. She was again a real star.

This took a great weight off the folks who had been following her. The Oaks and others were tired of having to try to catch up with an audience who had been ridden hard for over an hour. Tanya drained crowds and left them all but dead. She made life a living hell for those who had to follow her. No longer did people have to worry about that.

As Tanya's classy show hit the road in a large number of buses, as she and Presley settled into their home on wheels, and as Tanya hired and fired a large number of nannies, "My Arms Stay Open All Night" continued to climb up the charts. Its twenty-six-week tenure was the longest of Tanya's career. It stayed at #2 for two straight weeks. It was a big hit, just the kind she needed to kick off sales for her "Greatest Hits" album. And the LP did sell!

With everything seemingly working to push her away from the top, many wondered why Tanya was suddenly selling more than a standard one hundred thousand units. In the midst of a moral revolution led by television preachers and right-wing radio hosts, she was on fire in the Bible Belt and beyond. How was this possible?

First was the explosion in country music. It had been hinted at for generations. Eddy Arnold and Jim Reeves had crossed over into the city crowd in the late fifties and early sixties. Certainly Dolly Parton, Mac Davis and even Glen Campbell had made pushes before the eighties. Yet it was the establishment of the Nashville Network, the strong surge made by real country bands, and the network success of the NBC television show "Barbara Mandrell and the Mandrell Sisters," that seemed to have combined to really put wheels on the machine. Country music was not just the music of the rural people anymore, it was the music of all kinds of people. Artists like Alabama, Randy Travis, Reba McEntire and Garth Brooks had seized the advantage given to them and had opened the medium up to a whole new group of fans. These younger fans bought the product, and they bought it in larger numbers than ever before. This led to more money being placed into country music promotion and this led to even greater exposure and acceptance of that product.

In Tanya's case that was very important. Her former record labels had never done a good job promoting albums or placing them in stores. The support hadn't been there. They had let Tanya and her fans pump her product. Capitol was different. They were printing more product, shipping it out to every outlet they could find and working some magic with in-store displays. By their large presence in the marketplace they were making the statement that Tanya was hot. This forced their salespeople to hawk her product. This put the pressure on them to meet the number and print more. It was a cycle that literally fed itself.

The label had also begun to package Tanya as the

classy, sexy lady. They vowed to spend money, and Bob Freese, VP of sales and marketing made sure they did.

Finally, Tanya was becoming big in dance clubs and dance clubs were becoming the rage around the country. Much like rock 'n' roll had once been driven by new dances and dance music, country was now heading in that direction. A great deal of Tanya's music was easy to dance to, and this created even more buyers.

Still Tanya was waiting for her first platinum album. She had gold, but other country acts were now earning platinum and double platinum. She was a good seller, but she figured that to win a major award she was going to have to be up there at the top. What this meant to her was working harder than ever.

So each night on stage, day after day, city after city, she was smiling, wriggling her rear, pointing to fans, joking, and doing everything she could to not only have fun on stage, but to get the audience to really love her. She signed autographs, posed for pictures, gave out kisses and hugged old men. And whenever possible, she brought Presley out into the spotlight. The child was Tanya's crown jewel, she was the person Tanya most loved, and she wanted everyone to know that.

Tanya wore Presley like a medal. Presley seemed to have a great deal of natural ham in her. She ate up having her picture taken and loved having a fuss made over her by complete strangers. It was obvious she enjoyed the warm glow of the spotlight. But to stay in the spotlight one had to keep moving, and Tanya did a great deal of that. She woke up Branson at the Roy Clark Theater and shot over to L.A. to do a great dramatic role on the NBC television show "Shannon's Deal." Then it was back to Texas, the East Coast and then L.A.

She filmed a show that revived her love of animals. *Elephantastic* was shot at Marine World/Africa USA. During her few days on the set she rode elephants and played with wallabies, alligators, llamas, orangutans, pot-bellied pigs and camels. For the first time in almost a year, she looked rested, natural and seemed to be having a lot of fun. For the first time since becoming a mother she seemed as if she were a child again. So it was only natural for her to look back over her past when people talked to her on the set.

"People tell me I've missed a normal childhood and all that stuff, but I genuinely love being a celebrity." Then, even after thinking about all the hard work she challenged those around her by saying, "Most people would be more than happy to trade places with me anytime. They'd love to be Tanya Tucker." That may have been true, but few people would want to try to be a mother and keep up with Tanya's schedule.

Describing herself as being on a lifetime concert tour, she traveled with makeup people, hairstylists and hosts of musicians. Her homes were hotel rooms and she rarely got to enjoy any real fruits from her labor. She shopped whenever she got the chance, but often she never had an opportunity to get away from the tour and its demands long enough to wear the clothes she bought. And she refused to slow down.

Against the advice of those who informed her she was doing too much, she took on the job as the 1990 Spokeswoman of Tennessee's Camp Discovery for handicapped children. On very little notice she flew to Chicago to visit and expound single motherhood on "Oprah." Within hours she was back in front of thousands of screaming people. And still she pushed on. If she was doing all of this for sales results, it was working.

The "Tennessee Woman" album was released in April 1990. Three major hits would come from this work. The first was a classic single with a fun, upbeat video that seemed to echo Tanya's playful spirit in "Walking Shoes." If possible the next was even more fun.

T. Graham Brown, one of country music's most colorful and original characters, joined Tanya on the powerful duet "Don't Go Out." "Shoes" climbed the charts stopping only when it hit the third spot. "Don't Go Out" cracked the top ten and landed in the sixth position. This seemed to prove that while Glen Campbell hadn't held the duet magic to lift Tanya up the charts, she had no problem finding this formula with a relative newcomer like Graham.

Capitol had first capitalized on Tanya's most recent success by digging into the old Columbia/MCA vaults for material for the album "Greatest Hits Encore." This gave new Tanya fans or recent converts to country music a chance to hear much of her early stuff. "Encore" included "Delta Dawn," "Don't Believe My Heart Could Stand Another You," "San Antonio Stroll," "The Jamestown Ferry," "Here's Some Love," "Would You Lay With Me," "Blood Red and Goin' Down," "Pecos Promenade," "What's Your Mama's Name," and "Texas (When I Die)."

In October Tanya celebrated her thirty-second birthday by releasing "It Won't Be Me." The tune didn't quit motoring up Billboard's list until it equaled the "Don't Go Out"'s final score. It rested at #6, and in the current competitive mood of the country music industry Capitol couldn't have been more pleased. In something of a quirky surprise, many radio stations also played the flip side of "It Won't Be Me." This produced a double-sided hit with "Oh What It Did to Me" peaking at #12 in early spring of 1991.

In a move that may have surprised some of Nashville's more conservative crowd, Tanya was chosen to cohost the "TNN Music City News Country Award Show" with Alan Jackson. For a "reformed" party girl, there was nothing like an award show. It was a chance to dress up and try to out "fun" the next person. She called it a "big old party where you get to see all the friends you never see during the year." The question was, how many of the people who were acting as if they were

Tanya's close friends really were? She still had a host of backbiting enemies in her hometown. The tabloid press proved this almost every week.

In her spare time, and there was oh so little of it, she still rode horses. To emphasize just how good she still was she won the National Cutting Horse Association Third Annual Futurity Celebrity Cutting Horse Championship. Laughing she stated, "All I need is a good horse, a good man and a good song."

Her money had bought her a barnful of good horses, and she had a host of great songwriters now pushing her super songs, but she still hadn't found that good man. In an effort to get things together with her daughter's father, she did attempt to allow him more time in their lives. Reed, once a stranger in Nashville, was now a regular visitor. Some, including Beau, sensed that maybe this time the two would get together and tie the knot. The old man was partially right. They did get together from time to time, but they couldn't seem to tie the knot. Every time they got close they'd find a way to get at each other's throats again. Much like her days with Glen, Tanya was either lovin' or fightin'.

The lack of being able to win the big award and find a good man, someone who was as tough and steady as her father, seemed to frustrate Tanya. She could not win awards in spite of having big record after big record. Tanya told writers that she was still moving up the mountain. But her resolve might have been lagging a bit as she added, "When it's all over, I hope my music will play an important role in the overall scope of things for having been unique." This statement coming from the usually confident and assured Tanya seemed a sign of weakness. Her family was looking at the woman who once said that motherhood had completely fulfilled her and wondered if she wasn't heading back down a road too often traveled.

She told a reporter that she stayed in shape in a very

unusual fashion. Between sips of rum and Coke and long drags on a cigarette she proclaimed that her band's motto was sex, drugs and country music. She then laughed that you can "only take so many Excedrin P.M." Was she joking or not? Even those close to her didn't know.

The party girl image resurfaced as Tanya began leaving Presley at home rather than taking her on the road. The tabloids even quoted Beau as saying, "If she doesn't clean up her act, I'm seriously thinking of committing her somewhere and making her take care of herself."

Tanya's drinking was supposedly up. Was it? Why else would she look so tired? Why else would she seem so exhausted all the time? Why indeed!

Tanya and Ben had been off and on, on and off, and off and on again. She seemed to need him a few days and then not want him around for weeks at a time. When he wasn't around, she would audition other men. She was still looking for love, and like the old country song goes, looking in all the wrong places.

Finally, just when Beau had had about as much as he could stand, the family met in Vegas. With Ben Reed at her side Tanya announced to her parents that she was pregnant again. Reed stayed by her side for three days and even hinted that he wanted to set a wedding date. The fact that Reed didn't smoke, drink or do drugs gave both family and friends something about which they could pray. Maybe here was a man who would do Tanya some good. Her verdict was no. He was a great father, possessed a great gene pool, but he was definitely not the man she wanted to marry. At least not at this time.

With the rumor mill running wild that she was having problems with drugs and booze, Tanya opened up to the press. "The only problems I have are with ex-employees who start rumors that aren't true." She explained that while she was pregnant again, she really didn't have any problems. "I did have a drug problem with cocaine when I went into the Betty Ford Clinic in 1988," she pointed out. But she explained that since that time she had stayed off drugs completely. She credited her first pregnancy with helping her stay off and giving her a second chance at life. She also shrugged off the reports that she was an alcoholic. "Booze has never been a problem with me."

About the pregnancy Tanya was straightforward from the first. The father was "God's great gift. This guy is drop-dead gorgeous . . . And he's a great dad!" She also explained that she and the father planned this child and were very happy. She complimented Ben on being gentle, understanding and kind. She explained that while marriage would be nice, she had no such plans at this time.

"This is not the way I wanted it either," she admitted when quizzed about being pregnant again. "But I think the best role model, and I definitely want to be one, is that you gotta do what you feel makes you happy. How can you look at a child like Presley and say that's a mistake? I don't think I have messed up."

When asked if she was worried about her country music fans finally having their fill of her wicked ways and walking away, she shrugged her shoulders. "Country Music is changing. It's gettin' a lot hipper." If she was worried, she wasn't showing it.

Tanya had experienced a wonderful ride since giving birth to Presley. She had broken the top ten four times. So Capitol had every reason to believe that if they could get her at least one more major hit before the last round of voting for the CMA awards took place they might be able to push her to an award. Then Tanya had dropped the new bomb. With this pregnancy, the soon to be baby, the fact that she still wasn't getting married and the outrage it had aroused in some camps, Capitol had every right to be nervous. Would Tanya's career and all the hard work their team had done to put her in a position to challenge Reba McEntire go sliding down the tubes? Would critics and fans, as well as radio stations now stay away?

Tanya didn't seem to be concerned. She never won awards, and with the baby due in September, the show was hardly on her mind. This year she wouldn't even need to buy a dress or find a date. She was much more concerned with the new child, a son, and the fun she could have with him. As she shopped for little boy things she told all who would listen that the child's name would be Andrew Grayson Tucker. She also informed the world that having a baby boy fulfilled her biggest wish. It was too bad that she and Ben didn't work things out for a marriage, she admitted, but she did reach a goal of giving her daughter a full-blooded brother. So she was happy. The career really didn't matter that much.

Tanya was even beginning to talk about the days when she wouldn't be out on the road. "I don't want to be a struggling has-been ten years from now making ten percent of what I am making now. I want to go out in a blaze of glory or forget it." Would her son be her blaze? Some in country music thought so. Of course Tanya had never been too easy to predict.

Capitol released "Down to my Last Teardrop" in June. They probably shouldn't have been scared by Tanya's latest shocking news. Her fans seemed to be shockproof. "Teardrop" hit the ground running and picked up speed. It climbed to #2 and held there for two weeks before beginning its slide down. It was the sixth of twelve straight Tucker releases that would remain on the charts for at least twenty weeks.

Nashville was too busy getting ready for the award show to worry about Tanya and her child. Besides, she never won anyway, so it really wouldn't be a factor in the telecast. They would read her name a couple of times and then forget her. At least that was what most thought. Others believed differently, and while one prominent scribe was a long way from Music City, he wasn't afraid to raise his voice.

"Isn't it about time that Tanya Tucker gets the recognition she deserves?" asked Larry Delaney of *Country Music News* and The Voice of Country Music in Canada. "If it is really the music that counts, Tanya delivers it all." In the United States, most people didn't have the courage to agree with him.

As Tanya readied for her child's birth, "What Do I Do With Me" went Certified Gold then Platinum. It was the first Tucker Platinum ("TNT" and "Greatest Hits" only went gold). But that was just the beginning of the good news.

On the same day as the awards show, Tanya checked into the hospital, and with Ben Reed standing outside the delivery room door, gave birth to her son. As should have been predicted, she tossed people a curve and changed his name at the last minute. On the afternoon of October 2, 1991, she announced the arrival of Beau Grayson, named in honor of her father. Tanya thought she couldn't be more pleased.

Then on that evening, in a major upset, Tanya broke into the win column at the CMA. She was named the 1991 CMA Female Vocalist of the Year.

In the press room the announcement brought a huge standing ovation. "It was about damn time," said several in attendance. A few remained strangely silent. One muttered, "What the hell is going on when a slut can win a CMA award?"

The next day most radio stations around the country geared up to play a lot of Tanya's tunes. A few, feeling much the same way that the one reporter had, didn't. It was almost as if Tanya hadn't won at all. And that was the problem.

Tanya had been all right in the Bible Belt when she

was a bridesmaid. People could look at her never having been lifted to equal footing with Barbara Mandrell or Reba McEntire as poetic justice for living a sinful life. But now that she was a winner and had been put in the record books, they were beginning to wonder if country music had sunk to a level lower than they wanted to consider.

The next Sunday morning, as Tanya celebrated having her son, countless preachers picked up on this theme. They used Tanya's honor as a benchmark for questioning how low America had fallen. It seemed strange that in a business that sold hundreds of millions of records about drinking, cheating and lying, that a young woman could be condemned for having two children rather than aborting them and writing them off as mistakes. In many ways it seemed that the Bible Belt's and country music's values were just as inconsistent as Tanya's.

Chapter Fifteen

Great New Beginnings

[Tanya has] a voice that tears like a rusty saw blade.

—*Randy Lewis of the* Los Angeles Times

*F*or the sake of Tanya's image it would have been nice if she and the father of her children could have somehow fallen in love during the days right after their son's birth. Certainly they had the time, and with Tanya now finally being recognized as one of the best of the best, certainly theirs was a positive atmosphere to build on, so Beau and Juanita were hopeful.

"They are still talking about marriage," said Beau. But then he added, "I don't want her to get married just to get married. I want her to be married to somebody she can stay with." Her father's postscript said a great deal about just how much he wanted Tanya to experience the special love and bond that he and her mother had now known for almost half a century. Somehow he was beginning to believe that it was not a part of this relationship. The chemistry wasn't right. There was a caring, a physical attraction, but there wasn't magic. And without the magic, there wasn't going to be any love.

Tanya had told Beau on many occasions that no one could possibly measure up to him. Her father was her ideal man. She was looking for someone who had that much drive, that much love, that much backbone, and would sacrifice that much for her. As she had informed countless reporters for the past decade, "Daddy does everything from cleaning out my stables to handling my money. That makes him a hard act to follow." Hard act indeed, following Beau would be more like impossible. So this was what was facing Ben. He had to be everything Beau was, and then just a little more.

Reed came and stayed with Tanya and the children for three weeks. He helped Tanya as best he could, played with his daughter and admired his son. But when that time was over, so was Tanya's need for Reed. This time, with this child, he walked away knowing that the relationship between him and Tanya was healthier. While he was headed back to Los Angeles to try to pick up an acting career, he knew that Tanya would welcome him back whenever he felt a need to see the children. She wanted him in the children's lives. She felt that it was important for them to know their father. On the flip side, she didn't always want Ben in her life. Tanya believed that for the children's sake, this on and off again relationship was far healthier than one where there was a divorce and all the negative vibes that went with that action.

Reed might have been disappointed that they couldn't fall in love, and so too was her record label and anyone concerned with her public relations, but anyone who knew Tanya realized that she was not going to live a lie. She didn't love Ben Reed, and love was the only reason people got married. So, rather than waste time trying to fall in love with someone whom she hadn't been able to fall in love with over the past three years, it was time to meet someone new—a man who might measure up to Daddy.

Finding a new man was probably the last thing on her mind as the year wound down. She now had two children and she had to be thinking first and foremost of how she wanted to raise them. A lot of conversation with both the media and family concerned this topic.

She wanted them to be normal, she said again and again. She wanted them to be well-adjusted and happy. And she wanted them to have these qualities despite the fact that they were going to be raised on or around the road and with more money and things than most kids will ever have.

"I don't want my kids to grow up thinking we're rich," Tanya admitted. "I want them to feel rich on the inside." In a sense this statement gave a tremendous insight into Tanya's long struggle to find herself. Through both men, drugs and booze she had searched for a feeling that was as rich as the success she had found on records and in concerts. A feeling that was as high as the fans' adoration. Yet, much like Marilyn Monroe, there was a hollowness that came from being the financial bandwagon for a few hundred people and the idol and icon for a few million others. The price was loneliness. The price was living in a world where few people were completely honest with her.

Tanya Tucker was now a business—a big business. Because she was so successful, literally hundreds of people within her band, her organization, the record label, and other outside sources depended upon her for their living. Many of these people were so insecure that they would laugh at all her jokes, agree with her every view, and practically fall on their knees when she approached. Like other huge stars, she had entered the "Yes" world. In this land she was always right because no one would ever consider telling her she was wrong. Many in the business refer to this as "right by default." Behind her back there might be those who would say, "That's a stupid idea," but not in front of her. And for someone who was as honest as Tanya, the lack of honesty hurt.

She once lamented that she didn't care if her friends used her—she was more than happy to give them anything they wanted—but it hurt a great deal when they abused her. She hated that they went to the tabloids and sold stories that were based on private conversations. She hated that they would not be honest when she needed their advice. Tanya may have been tough on the outside, but she was very sensitive on the inside. Under her occasional outbursts of anger and rage were tears. And yet in the face of being hurt time and time again, she never quit forgiving and giving. She needed real friends that badly.

For most of Tanya's life, mostly because she was in the public eye, subtle as well as frightening abuse came from people who claimed they cared for her. It was this "abuse of the heart and trust" that hurt most deeply. It was this abuse that made her want to retreat and probably contributed to her not wanting to trust a man enough to marry him. Would he betray her like many of her friends and past employees had?

In that very real sense Tanya was as much a victim of her fame as Elvis and Marilyn, and while her excesses could not be excused, put in that light they could at least be understood. Tanya needed insulation, and who could fault her for looking in some of the wrong places to find it. Yet, unlike Elvis and Marilyn, she now had children around her who allowed her to focus on something more positive than the loneliness of the top.

Her 1991 Christmas card showed her dogs, the kids, Santa and Tanya. Yet as sweet as the picture was, what probably meant the most was the message inscribed on the inside, "Great New Beginnings."

With an award of her own, this was a chance for her to really begin again. So she rode through the "slut" mentality that surfaced just after she won her award and skated into the new year with a new attitude and new outlook. Gone was the "Ms. Bad Ass," license plate. Her new one read, "Miss T."

This sensitive Tanya looked at her children and realized how fragile life really was. She addressed that as much as she talked about her music or the honor of finally wining an award.

"I know a mother who lost her twelve-year-old daughter to a viral infection," Tanya whispered during a press junket. "My God, if that happened to me, I don't know what I would do. You just get so attached." From there she went off into a discussion about the state of schools and the environment. She was so concerned that children of this new generation would not have a chance to really enjoy the wonders of childhood and beauties of the world.

And for the first time she wistfully dreamed about taking a world tour. This time she didn't want to work concerts, she wanted to see things. Tanya wanted to visit Africa and Australia to view the wildlife. She wanted to dive off the Great Barrier Reef. In the past she might have hated the tours because it took time away from partying. Now she wanted some free time to enjoy the wonders of the world. Having a good time meant something vastly different than it used to.

Having two children had not hurt her image enough to discourage companies from approaching her for endorsements. One that she chose harkened back to her childhood and the times spent in the wide open deserts of the southwest. When the Stetson Hat Company asked her to endorse a line of ladies' hats, it seemed a perfect fit. For starters, Tanya looked great in a cowboy hat. Yet more importantly, cowboy hats had been a natural part of her whole life. She had seen them everywhere. And, as she had said many times, she loved cowboys.

As she pushed into the year, Tanya also discovered that Stetson wasn't the only one who loved her. By and large the media did too. Part of it was her willingness to do interviews. She was as open, honest and available as she had been before she became a star and again when she was trying to climb back up the ladder. She was natural and compassionate, very patient with each reporter. The smile and sparkle and glow were there brighter than ever before. She was fun, but not mean-spirited. She gave great answers, but she wouldn't put people down. This was especially clear when she informed reporters that she had learned a great deal about the business from Glen Campbell. This hardly sounded like country music's bad girl. Yet that image was still around and still working in her favor.

She was actually profiled as one of country music's all-time great outlaws. The list was made up of fifteen people. The only women to join the likes of David Allen Coe, Hank Williams and Johnny Paycheck, were Jessi Colter, who made it by default, k.d. lang, who would have probably hit near the top without having announced that she was a lesbian, and Tanya Tucker.

Tanya was the one lady of the current crop of performers who should have been on the list because of her history. She had lived outside establishment circles. With two children without benefit of marriage, she still did, but she wasn't the outlaw she had once been. So in a sense, this "Hall of Fame" award may have been passed out a bit too late. But those who composed it must have known that Tanya still had a few tricks up her sleeve. It would just take a while for them to surface. Tongues might be still now, but she would make them wag again. They were confident.

With an award in the pocket and an artist who seemed committed to working the road and creating more magic, Capitol settled on "Down to my Last Teardrop" as her next release. "Last Teardrop" would earn a nomination for a Grammy, and when it peaked in June the song was #2. It was backed by a delightful, sexy, playful Tanya video that was as catchy as the tune itself. This again proved that Tanya knew how to use television to her best advantage.

Outside of Nashville people hadn't caught the "new"

Tanya. They were still comparing the country superstar to rock shockers like Madonna. This was a comparison that probably made Tanya laugh. Tanya's value system may have been a strange jumble of both conservative and liberal values, she may have once partied hard and long, but she never washed all of her laundry in public. She never stood before the cameras nude begging people to take photos of her. She never was crude during live interviews. Tanya had a limit. Tanya had pride and self-respect. Tanya may have been maturing a bit more slowly than Reba McEntire or Barbara Mandrell, but she was far more mature than Madonna when she was recording "Delta Dawn."

The rock diva may have picked up on this because Madonna sneered at Tanya during a West Coast awards dinner. The goddess of shock waited until the cameras were pointing at her to dish out her scathing expression. Meanwhile, Tanya shrugged back with a "what is the matter with you look."

Madonna was probably hoping for a bit more. In the old days it might have meant a cat fight, but these weren't the old days. The rock star's glare was questioned only with a whisper to a friend from Tanya. "I wonder why she did that? I've never done anything to her."

No one will probably ever know why Madonna mugged for the press, but it might have been jealousy that fueled the move. After all, only one country act could possibly challenge Madonna and the press's love affair with her. That person was Tanya. Madonna had to have feared that the country star could push the rock princess off the front page of the rags almost anytime she wanted. But for now, Tanya couldn't have cared less. Sparring with the "Queen of Shock" didn't interest her. This probably infuriated Madonna even more than a public fight.

As Tanya continued to tour and turn heads with her slim look and confidence, she also continued to turn out hits. "(Without You) What Do I Do About Me" was her next single. It was off the same album, "What Do I Do With Me," that had given birth to Tanya's latest hit "Down to my Last Teardrop."

"What Do I Do With Me" was a haunting song that hit people in the heart and left them cold. When love leaves you, what will you do about your life? Some thought that Tanya sang it with such conviction because she lived it every day. They wanted to believe that Ben Reed was the villain and that he had broken her heart. The truth was that Tanya simply gave a great, gut-wrenching performance and drove the cut up the charts to #2. For now neither Reed nor any other man could touch her heart.

When CMA awards time came around, Tanya was again nominated, but this time she didn't get a chance to win. It didn't bother her at all. Why not? With an award on her shelf at home, it wasn't a question that concerned her. That first award had signaled the acceptance that she needed. Besides, there were fresh players in the industry, and she honestly felt that they deserved to taste some success too.

While many of the recent old-timers were quaking in their boots wondering how long their options would be picked up by their labels, "T" was as casual as ever. "I think it's great [new blood]," Tanya explained. "They make country music even better. I'm really proud of country music right now. I mean, I've always been proud of it. It's just getting better and better." Tanya was one of the reasons it was getting better and better. While her sales alone proved this, a host of critics backed it up with glowing words of tribute.

In 1992 David Zimmerman of *USA Today* wrote about the "Can't Run From Yourself" album, "This

Texas born star's personality infuses every note with sexy radiance."

James M. Tarbox of *Knight-Ridder* also commented on Tanya's newest album with a glowing tribute. "On this moody collection Tucker is in fine voice—bluesy, growly, and ragged. It's fine whether she's belting out a blues honky-tonker or caressing a weepy ballad."

Randy Lewis of the *Los Angeles Times* chimed in, ". . . a voice that tears like a rusty saw blade."

Not to be outdone, the *Chicago Tribune* added, "One of country music's greatest and most distinctive vocalists: raw throated blues, playful sexiness. Tucker brings guts and style to not only singing but living."

People magazine had been on Tanya's bandwagon for years. Now they explained why in precise, well-chosen words. "Tucker's got Mack-truck longevity. Mack-truck vocal power, too. One-third tawdry, two-thirds talent: just the right proportions for a full-grown country diva."

The *Indianapolis Star* harkened back to her days of searching in rock when they reviewed her. "Sensual rawness with a touch of rock and roll and a thread of introspection." Could she gain any more kudos? Hundreds! Far too many to find room to be glued into her scrapbooks.

The *Tribune*'s Jennifer Tucker hit it when she gushed, "Tucker's husky vocals are some of the most recognizable pipes in country music, a kind of take-that-you-rascal sound. The defiance is there in the growl, the honesty is there in the hush. She's an independent woman who isn't afraid to be the same way on stage. That alone is worth a round of applause."

So maybe Madonna had picked up on the fact that this woman had everything the rock star thought she had claimed a patent on, plus Tanya now had respectability. Tanya had also experienced forgiveness, and that was even rarer.

Could things get any better? Had Tanya now reached

a point where she had peaked out and would begin her slide down? Was Ms. Tucker finally tamed? Music City was feeling secure, but they should have known better than to turn their backs on a tiger!

- Chapter Sixteen -

Two Sparrows

I hear she's a very nice girl.

—Dan Quayle

*T*anya's life had changed a great deal since her early childhood days on the road. She was no longer relying on one hit song to sell concert tickets, she had dozens. She no longer had to use a house band, she had one of the tightest, best dressed groups on the circuit. She no longer had to worry about lights or sound, her system was state of the art. And she no longer had to hold on tight in the backseat of a well-worn Cadillac as she and her father raced to a show date. She now had several buses, a tour manager, a lighting and stage manager, the band, a wardrobe director, a nanny and a fleet of drivers. Her personal bus was forty-five feet long, sported a full bed, a refrigerator and full kitchen, a washer and dryer, a shower, full video and audio setups, a sun deck and a sliding door like something out of *Star Trek*. In 1972 she had arrived on the scene, but twenty years later she had "arrived." It had been a long time coming, but she had come a long way in that time!

One thing hadn't changed much over those two decades. In 1972 she worked around the clock and pushed as many as two hundred dates a year. In 1992 Tanya still worked nonstop pushing more than two hundred dates a year. Once she worked for fame and recognition, now she said she was working strictly for the money.

"I'm going to give it all away," she said laughing, "and I sure ain't going to die with a bunch of it." And she was again honest. Few people knew how to spend money as well as Tanya. She had a beautiful new farm and home in Tennessee, a handful of cars, a barnful of horses and closets full of clothes. She had so many outfits that she could probably never wear them all.

But she had another passion beside buying things for herself and her kids. Like her hero Elvis, Tanya loved giving things away. If she was shopping and she noted one of her friends studying an outfit, she bought it for them. If someone commented on how much they liked something in her closet, she pulled it out and gave it to them. She loved giving. It seemed to be as much a passion with her as singing or partying.

On stage was the same. Night after night, doing the same show, singing the same songs, she still loved giving to her fans. They came to see her move, and she moved even when she was sick and didn't feel like it. They came to see her sing, and she tore into songs even when her throat was raw and bleeding. They came to get her autograph or picture, and she signed and posed whenever she had the time.

Maybe for that reason—at a time when critics were getting tired of other acts—they still seemed to write great things about her. They sensed that she might not have the production numbers that Reba did, but she sure would sweat in order to let the people see and hear her soul. They loved her for that.

And so while other contemporaries had drifted off to semiretirement, ceased recording or opened theaters in Branson, she was still being followed and photographed. Television constantly called, and sometimes she listened and accepted the invitations. She whooped it up on "Arsenio Hall," spoke quietly and sincerely on "CBS This Morning," laughed and shared mothering secrets on "The Home Show," poked fun and teased on "John &

Leeza," and was the country queen for "Entertainment Tonight." Tanya on the tube was special, so the networks, cable spots and magazine shows put her on their semiregular list. She was making other lists too!

In 1992 Tanya was one of *People*'s "10 Best Dressed People of 1992." That was some kind of honor for a woman who used to be labeled "Nashville's Trash Queen." She now had style, and a whole bunch of clothing companies were after her to design a line of country clothes for them.

All the adulation, all the attention, all the fame, combined with the joy of watching her children grow up, often made the singer look back over her own life and question why and how things had come together as they did. She often wondered, what if it hadn't worked out the way it did? Where would she be now?

"I often wonder what would have happened to my career if I hadn't had Billy Sherrill as my first producer," she admitted during conversations.

It was Billy who sensed that her strong suit was the story-songs that defined the first stage in her career. If he had tried to get her to do straight love songs or little-girl-cute numbers, she probably wouldn't have made it. Of course if Sherrill hadn't brought her over to Glen Campbell's house for a sing-along, the middle portion of her life might have been much different too.

"I'd love to do another album with him someday," Tanya admitted to Dave Hoekstar of the *Chicago Metropolitan Area* as she looked back on those early days in the Columbia studios with Billy. "I think we kind of turned country music around. We gave it a little jab in the arm. They were all in shock."

This looking back often caused Tanya to venture a glance ahead too. She wondered what others would think about her when her career had passed. She hoped that her country music legacy would be a tribute to her staying power, not her tabloid image.

"Hopefully, when it is over and done with, they'll say that I had longevity and that I hung in there." If she stopped even at this moment, no one would deny her that.

Once Tanya probably thought that being the "Female Elvis" would make her the most important person on earth. Now after twenty years and a couple of comebacks, she had put together a new perspective. Being a singer was not all it was cracked up to be.

"Anybody can sing," she told several members of the press, "if I could cure cancer, then I'd say I've done something important."

It seemed strange that when she really made it to the top Tanya began to realize that the zenith was not all it was cracked up to be. Her main goal now was to be a mother. She wanted to do that job as well as she thought her own mother had. Yet now she seemed to fully realize that the pressure exerted on someone in the spotlight was ten times greater than on a normal woman or mother. Her biggest problem was not having enough hours in the day.

"I'm constantly doing stuff," she would complain when the days ended late and she was worn down to the bone. "Interviews, promotions, meetings, traveling. Some of my friends come out on the road with me and they're amazed at the things that are done and the pace that we keep. They just can't believe it. Everyone has the wrong idea about the life of an entertainer—we don't have anything to do. It's really kind of funny when I think about all the things I actually do. The performance is probably the easiest part of it." It was surely a lot easier than being a mother.

She told friends who were worried that the pace was too frantic, "Sleep is something I used to do." So was playing. She didn't seem to have time for either. Such was success's high price.

Looking at her children while they played or slept she

would whisper, "My most fervent prayer is that they will survive all of this. I know I will. . . ." But there had to be times when she wondered how long she could keep up two hundred nights on the road each year.

Besides her lack of time with her own children, Tanya also was becoming convinced that time on the road was killing her chance to ever have a deep, committed relationship with a man. There was not time to really date. There was so little time to get to know someone new. Most men she met quickly grew impatient with having to wait until she got the business side of things taken care of. By the time she finished, they were gone.

"I'm a good-hearted person," she told those around her. But they already knew that. They knew what she really meant was that she wanted someone to share the wonderful things of her life with, but she was afraid that she would never find someone who could measure up to her standards. There wasn't time and her life was laid out in a way to make it impossible. This hurt her greatly, more than she would ever let on to anyone, including her family.

"I believe in Daddy and he believes in me," she constantly said when explaining their relationship. This mirrored what he had verbalized some two decades before. Then she added, as she had a hundred times before, "He's the reason I'm not married yet." In one sense she meant that no one could measure up to her father. Yet it also went deeper than that.

She told the *Star* the rest of the story. "My daddy intimidates most men I know. I'd like a guy who's man enough to say to him, 'I love your daughter. That's it!'"

Close friends echoed her desire to for a man who would stand up and be a man—a John Wayne kind of guy. Yet at the same moment she talked about her ideal and confessed she dreamed of being a typical forever-and-ever kind of wife, she also admitted that she had never felt easy about settling down. What could settle her uneasiness? The answer would seem to be a man whom she did not intimidate, one she could not control. But was there anyone who could control Tanya?

Over the course of her life only a few men had ever won Tanya's trust. Jerry Crutchfield had, so too had Billy Sherrill. And after a long trial period, so had Liberty Record's Jimmy Bowen. Bowen was well-known and respected around Nashville, and Tanya had felt that he had done a great job with her at Capitol. Now, even though a business venture had switched the label's name to Liberty, she felt that Bowen had a good concept as to who she was and how best to position her in his stable of acts.

This confidence had been earned because he had stuck with her through some very sticky times. Some folks would have quickly turned their back on her during her first illegitimate birth. The second would have caused Music City to slam the door and throw away the key. But not Jimmy. He had given her the benefit of the doubt. He had continued to push her. And it had paid off.

Her bio now stated, "She's one of the finest song stylists to ever grace a Nashville recording studio, capable of taking any writer's material and making it irrevocably her own. Once Tanya Tucker has recorded a song she owns the patent on it. She's also one of the most diverse artists in the business, capable of moving from gutsy blues to two-steppin' honky-tonk to mournful ballad in the blink of an eye. . . . Tanya Tucker is one of country music's treasures: a singer who imposes her lively personality on everything she sings and every show she performs." Jimmy didn't write the words, but he believed them.

Bowen was acutely aware of the fact that in a day when so many artists were mirror images of each other, when so many acts sounded so much like another, that Tanya was vastly different. She was one of the few whose

voice and style were so identifiable, that anyone who
turned on a radio knew it was Tanya the second they
heard her voice. That was power, and he was willing to
risk a bit of moral criticism to hold onto it.

Tanya's next hit was "Some Kind of Trouble." The
song's title echoed the sentiments of many who had
worked with Tanya in various times during her check-
ered career. Certainly she had been some kind of trouble, but the song had no problems. It was a perfect
growling upbeat tune in Tanya's unique style. With Jerry
Crutchfield at the controls, the two had again found the
key to keeping people purchasing the product and disc
jockeys spinning hits. "Trouble" hit on February 15,
1992, and stayed around for twenty weeks, fading only
after it had scaled the heights to #3. The video oozed
sex appeal. No wonder it remained in heavy rotation
long after the single had fallen off the music charts.

To fully mine the richness of Tanya's latest incredible
album, Capitol/Liberty then pegged "If Your Heart
Ain't Busy Tonight" as the fourth single. It too lasted
twenty weeks, beginning hot in May and scorching the
charts until four months later when it peaked at #4.
CMA's top female was solid gold, and Capitol wanted
to capitalize on that face at every turn.

Branson, Missouri, had been changing and climbing
upward almost as fast as Tanya. Like the singer's rapid
rise, the Ozark Mountain country music mecca's growth
had caught Nashville by surprise. Many of Music City's
top acts were now joining the Opry old-timers and playing a number of their prime dates in Branson. The
newly constructed Grand Palace, already dubbed as
"Country Music Carnegie Hall," wanted to welcome
Tanya to the hill country. They teamed her for a week
with one of their hosts, Louise Mandrell. Their other
host, Glen Campbell, was for some reason out of town.

The younger Mandrell sister had the highest energy
shown in town. Other entertainers often avoided work-

ing the Palace when she was in town simply because they didn't want to follow her. Tanya, with her equally high energy entertainment-first drive, was the perfect second act. Between the two women they wore out twelve crowds in six days. As reviewers noted, these two singers left each audience completely drained. Those in the Mandrell/Tucker crowd who attended other Branson shows seemed bored. And why not, they had watched two people who thrived on the stage.

Mandrell, who had honed live entertainment as a craft in Vegas a few years before and had just recently turned down a shot a taking her show to Broadway, watched almost all of Tanya's shows from out in the audience. Louise stated admiringly, "Tanya is one of the best entertainers around. She works hard and gives it up for the audience." This had been more than obvious for that week. When Campbell rode back into town the next week, his show seemed tame by comparison.

As Tanya left the Ozarks and hunkered into her summer tour package, she couldn't have guessed just how eventful or how strange the summer of 1992 was going to be. Beyond her world of family and entertainment, the nation's focus was on a battle for the presidency between a Washington insider and a Southern outsider. It was a scrape between a man who was pushing traditional family values and one battling rumors of extramarital affairs. It was pro-choice against pro-life, women's rights against male dominated, old-fashioned government, big business fighting it out with the rights of the individual. It was the old preworld war generation versus the baby boomer crowd. In the midst of this fray was a man from her now home state of Tennessee who would become a vice presidential nominee running against a man whom Tanya had openly ridiculed for his stand against single motherhood. Even though the singer was probably far too busy singing and being a mother to notice, this national political fight mirrored in many ways the long fight which Tanya herself had waged against the country music establishment. It was an outside rebel against the established inside power.

Logic would have dictated that Ms. Tucker would have lined up on the side of the more liberal and untraditional of the two choices. As was always the case, predicting the path of "The Texas Tornado" was a risky business. Tanya jumped on the Bush bandwagon and they embraced her.

On the Wednesday of the Republican National Convention in Houston, Texas, it was "Family Values" night. In a unique bit of booking strategy, Lee Greenwood, who was working on his fifth marriage, opened for the Grand Old Party faithful with the Pledge of Allegiance. Then Tanya Tucker, with her two children out of wedlock, came on to add music to this celebration of traditional Judeo/Christian virtues. This was the same Tanya Tucker who earlier in the year had said, "Who is Dan Quayle to go after single mothers? What in the world does he know of what it's like to go through pregnancy and have a child with no father for the baby? Who is he to call single mothers tramps?"

Quayle's press folks had then shot back, "It is reasonable to ask the entertainment industry to help provide leadership in turning around a deteriorating social situation."

At that time Tanya wanted a piece of Quayle, but he backed off. Then, when President Bush asked her to come to the convention, she took him up on it. The irony of her performance probably didn't hit her until she saw the "Family Values" banners and buttons.

When Tanya finished, the thrice-married and then separated Louise Mandrell took over. She wowed them with topflight work. She then handed the mike to Randy Travis.

Travis came closest to the kind of entertainer the GOP wanted to spotlight on this night. He had been married only once, had no illegitimate children, and had never been divorced. Of course it was public knowledge that he had lived with his new bride for several years before reciting any vows and that his wife was many years his senior. This was a bill made to order for the tabloids.

In another irony, the Republicans booked newly divorced Sandi Patti to sing the next evening. There seemed to be little doubt that this was a confused political party. It stood up for something and then embraced something else. There was little wonder that the wheels came off the machine before it ever left the station. Still, one thing had been proven. Country music was now at the heart and soul of almost everything American. Its popularity was unchallenged. And Tanya was still on the way up after twenty years!

"Being in country music is more exciting today than ever before," she stated in the middle of her 1992 tour. "Country music is so much more in the mainstream. A lot of young people have come over to country music for a lot of different reasons, our music is much better and our song appeal has much wider appeal and there are a lot of cute younger guys and gals making country music."

The Country Music Association again remembered her around her birthday. The CMA gave Tanya an award nomination for top Female Vocalist.

In October of 1992, Tanya's last Capitol album was released. "Can't Run From Yourself" proved to contain a great deal of gold. The first single, "Two Sparrows in a Hurricane" was just the right song at just the right time. Certainly Tanya's life had always appeared to be a hurricane. With all her success and longevity she had certainly passed the tornado status and jumped up on the storm gauge over tropical depression. She was now one of Music City's most powerful hit producers. In this song she had a soul mate, its title defined her career and its message spoke to her ideals. The latter were much closer to those expressed on the Republican's Family Values night than most people would ever guess.

The single "Two Sparrows in a Hurricane" jumped on the charts in September of 1992 and flew steadily up the charts for twenty weeks. It peaked like two of Tanya's last four releases at #2. By all accounts its power and force made it a song that should have earned the top position. It was a song that made people think, made them cry, and made them treasure the true love they had found.

The video would hit #1, and its effect would even be greater than the single's. A few months down the road, the West Coast version of the CMA, the Academy of Country Music, would award *Two Sparrows in a Hurricane* with its highest video honor. But even if the video hadn't earned that recognition, this was a special project for Tanya.

"Two Sparrows in a Hurricane" featured both of her children and their father, Ben Reed. Tanya was also able to get Mae Axton to play the lead role of the older woman who had loved a man for her entire life. In a haunting scene Tanya looked at Reed as she held both of their children. Everyone who knew her and loved her wished that these two wayward souls (Reed and Tanya) could somehow live out the story of this Mark Alan Stringer song. As the words promised, "The world says they'll never make it, but love says they will." If only it had been that simple and those words could come true. Yet rather than ideals, this piece of video was just another talked about bit in the continuing saga of Tanya's soap opera life.

Liberty Home video felt that the film's message was so strong it took the unusual measure of having it closed captioned for the hearing impaired. Everyone could agree that from first note to final fade-out, this was one of Tanya's finest pieces of work. Therefore, when she won the award it did mean a great deal to Tanya. Yet is was for reasons that the casual viewer would have never guessed that tears appeared in Tanya's eyes when she accepted the trophy.

"I just thought of my parents," she would gush. "Their fiftieth anniversary was a big reason I said I had to do this song. They were fifteen when they got married. They have been through so much together. My parents deserve this honor a lot more than I do. They have lived it!"

Beau and Juanita had to be thinking, if only Tanya could too.

- Chapter Seventeen -

Black Velvet Lady

Though Tucker's Elvis-like moves are tame by current pop standards, the thirty-five-year-old singer remains refreshingly unique in the country field.

—*Jay Orr*

Many of the members of the GOP who watched Tanya perform on their "Family Values" show and pretended that she had been reborn and reformed, must have been a bit taken back at the beginning of the new year. Of course if the Rupublican party was shocked, consider the staff at the Betty Ford Clinic and once again the Music City Establishment when Black Velvet Canadian Whiskey announced that Tanya Tucker would be the next model in all of their advertising. If this wasn't enough, the company would also sponsor her tour and a national country dance contest using Tanya as their spokesperson. As rumbles raced up and down the Cumberland River, Nashville again realized that children and the passing years were not going to stop Tanya Tucker from shocking them once again.

Being asked to be the "Black Velvet Lady," would have been considered quite an honor in most circles. Tanya was following a host of supermodels whose faces were known the world over. Christie Brinkley, Kim Alexis and Cheryl Tiegs had all been featured in countless magazines and on the cover of the famous *Sports Illustrated* swimsuit edition. These tall blondes were legends. They had their own clothes lines, were regulars on the talk show circuits, had sold millions of posters, had been escorted and courted by some of the world's best-looking and richest men and had grown in stature as they grew in years. Cybill Shepard, the other very well known "Black Velvet Lady," had jumped from modeling into a very successful career as an actress and singer. Like Tanya, she had suffered a bit in the tabloid press, but she had bounced back time and time again. Keeping company with this quartet of women was a huge leap in stature for the petite country singer.

As a part of the deal, Tanya would begin to wear more black velvet, appear in glamorous ads in publications such as *Playboy* and *Esquire*, and carry the company banner with her wherever she toured. In return Black Velvet would sponsor 250 show dates over a two-year period of time.

Liberty quickly jumped on the bandwagon by giving away sampler cassettes in an agreement with Black Velvet. The minitapes contained four of Tanya's hits with the whiskey company's logo on the box. As the two corporate giants moved forward and put their crossmarketing plans into action, Tanya's new sophisticated image began to come together.

Smooth Steppin's, the handle they decided upon for the dance contest, would raise money for the National Multiple Sclerosis Society. All entry fees would go directly to the organization for research. Liberty executives figured that this would deflect some of the criticism Tanya had initially received for falling under the endorsement of the whiskey company. And it was no secret that the initial press and public jibes had been tough. This marriage had upset everyone from Mothers Against Drunk Driving to booking agents. Fans were confused too.

Working against Tanya was her own history of abuse. She had been to the Betty Ford Clinic. While she had always maintained that she had gone into treatment for a drug problem, many experts believed that alcohol and drug abuse were linked. These experts could point to the times when Tanya had been a less than responsible consumer of alcoholic beverages. Was she being mature or responsible in promoting a product that might even be at the root of many of her highly publicized personal problems? Among many, including some of her strongest supporters the answer seemed to be a resounding "No!"

All the negative talk and press didn't seem to faze Tanya. She pointed out to the press that she was National Ambassador for MS. Every one of the tens of thousands of five-dollar entry fees for the Smooth Steppin's dance contest would go toward MS research. She maintained that she got involved with Black Velvet because they offered her a way to help people in her age range who had been hit by this terrible disease. With an opportunity to do so much for MS how could she turn her back on this opportunity? she inquired.

Not stopping with the plea for funds for research for one of America's most common cripplers of young adults, she also hit the road to speak about drinking responsibly. She didn't push the sponsor's product as much as informed those who did drink, to not drive or abuse alcohol. She also told all who were concerned by her association with the product that Black Velvet actually opened up a chance for her to preach to young people about how and when to use alcohol. Without this sponsor, the opportunity just wouldn't be there, she argued.

It was probably much ado about nothing. Tanya's new crowd had a great many of the same rebellious streaks in them that she did, so they didn't care. And those other fans, the ones who had been with her through the years, had already forgiven her for so many different things, what was one more?

So with nationally known dance instructor, Patsy Swayze, creating the Smooth Steppin's dance steps,

Tanya hit the road in a black velvet hat. In spite of what at first looked like a real problem, things couldn't have been smoother.

With "Sparrows" still hovering on the charts, Capitol Records was now completely under the Liberty banner. It was on the Liberty label that "It's a Little Too Late" was released. The Pat Terry and Roger Murrah cut, as always produced by Jerry Crutchfield, lasted twenty weeks on the charts, again hitting the second position, this time in the late summer of 1993. It was rereleased as a very successful dance club single later in the year.

"Tell Me About It," a duet with Delbert McClinton, proved commercial in a big way and became the ninth straight Tucker release to stay on the charts exactly twenty weeks. The star was now combining productivity and consistency. This meant real profits for Liberty. Only Garth Brooks sold more for them.

It was amazing to many that Tanya Tucker's sales punch was now much greater than Barbara Mandrell's, Loretta Lynn's and Tammy Wynette's had been in their primes. But such was the case. Of her last twelve releases, only one had failed to reach as high as the sixth place finish of "It Won't Be Me." That cut, "Oh What It Did to Me," finished in the top twenty and just off the top ten at #12. Of her twenty-two Capitol releases, dating back to her first single in 1986, *One Love at a Time*, all the other singles besides "Oh What It Did to Me" had made it at least to #8. Few modern acts, outside of the supergroup Alabama, could even begin to claim such domination. Over that same period of time, the reigning country music queen, Reba McEntire, had been shut out of the top ten on three occasions. Yes, Capitol's big gamble was paying off long after folks had forgotten that signing Tanya Tucker had ever been a gamble.

In May, in an almost unprecedented move when dealing with a young, living artist, the label made Tanya's first official Liberty album release her fourth greatest hits collection. "Greatest Hits 1990–1992" proved to the world just how successful Tanya had been in the first part of country music's greatest decade. If anyone doubted her contribution or status as one of country music's greatest of all times, all they had to do was look at the success of these cuts.

At about the same time that "Greatest Hits 1990–1992" was flying off the shelves, "What Do I Do About Me" and "Can't Run From Yourself" both went platinum. To say that Tanya was pleased was an understatement. "It's about time," she said smiling when she got the news. With the platinum albums another one of Tanya's long-held goals had been accomplished. Now everything she touched seemed to be coming up in an even more precious metal than gold. If only she could find a man with that platinum touch.

Tanya's lack of steady male companionship didn't come about from lack of trying. She was seen trying out new men almost every time she had a few days off. A twenty-seven-year-old Spanish model, Frank Chacon, caught her eye for a while. They even stayed at the singer's favorite romantic retreat in the desert, the Elvis Presley suite at the Las Vegas Hilton. Yet the Latin lover soon lost his fizzle and Tanya tossed him back to the other hungry women.

Young—*young* being the operative word—Matt Thurston, twenty-two and heir to Kentucky Fried Chicken, got together with Tanya first in Fort Lauderdale and later in the Bahamas. Thurston had met and fallen hard for Tanya at a hunting lodge in Maine while Tanya was working. After work they played for a while, but it was another relationship that just didn't pan out.

In between all the new men she was still seen sometimes with Ben Reed. Reed would admit that he was jealous of Tanya's other relationships, but stopping her from doing what she wanted to do would have been "like roping a whirlwind." At this point Reed just wasn't up to it.

Between her grinding tour schedule, her pumping Black Velvet and the dance contest around the country, the work in the studio, being a single mom on the road and at home, and her social life, Tanya was wearing down. She was trying to go like she had when she was a teenager and she found she just couldn't keep up anymore. And around every corner there seemed to be a new kind of trouble.

In the early part of the year Tanya was allegedly stalked by a forty-one-year-old Texan. Tanya had been threatened many times in her career. When she was young the kidnapping threats had been taken seriously enough that her brother Don accompanied her everywhere. Back then she was never alone. Recently, with the newfound success, the crackpots had again come out.

This was the worst. The man was arrested on May 14, 1993, after allegedly making threatening statements and actions concerning both the singer and her children. With his calls, he was becoming more and more frightening. Tanya notified authorities who did what they could. Still she was frightened. What if he grabbed her children when she was away? What if he hurt someone in her family? What if he was crazy enough to do something dangerous?

Then there were the logical questions she couldn't answer. How did he keep getting her unlisted number? When she changed it, how did he get the new one? If she didn't get together with him, might he kill her? Could she end it by just facing him down?

This situation was grating on her nerves worse than any amount of tabloid press. This was not what a single mother of two wonderful, but very small children needed.

The pressure from threats caused Tanya to put more

pressure on her nanny. The woman was number seven. The other six couldn't take Tanya's strict demands even before a crazy man entered the picture. If the children were on the road with her, then Tanya didn't want them out of her sight unless she was on stage. And as she sang she couldn't help but wonder if the nanny was protecting them like she would have. And where was the loon tonight?

He was finally picked up by authorities in late spring. He was deemed very confused and incompetent and was finally confined for a time to Middle Tennessee Mental Health Institute, although ultimately the criminal charges against him were dropped. With him behind locked doors Tanya could breathe easier, but now she knew what Barbara Mandrell, Reba McEntire and a host of other country music mothers had known for some time; there were a lot of crazies out there. While they once didn't seem too important, now that Tanya had kids, these people were much more terrifying!

If the worry of death threats weren't enough, the tabloids, still hot on her trail, reported it wasn't work or worry that was killing Tanya, it was her active social life. They wrote about a party life that would have killed three women. The mere fact that she didn't have time to party that hard didn't seem to keep people from believing that all the stories were completely accurate. The fact was that Tanya was simply trying to do more than she could do, and the weeks off with the new men in her life were not the way for her to get the rest she needed. But at times Tanya needed men as badly as she needed rest. This was just human nature.

If reports from friends were right, on the road and on vacations, the pressure was now getting to Tanya. She was smoking too much, still drinking some, and not eating properly. It was the bad eating habits and the lack of rest that did her in in the first part of the summer.

In early June, Tanya canceled a number of her tour

dates due to exhaustion. Beau would break the news to the press, the ticket holders and the bookers. "As a result of her hectic schedule, Tanya is physically exhausted and suffering from sleep deprivation. We sincerely regret that several shows will have to be postponed, but Tanya's health is our first priority."

Some newspapers wrote that Tanya was much sicker than had been reported. None seemed to offer her any sympathy. She was drilled time and time again. This drilling led to her ending her time off far too soon. Tanya ended the speculation by again hitting the road after only a few days in bed.

It was obvious from the first show that she had come back too soon. Her shows were shorter and even the band questioned just what was wrong with her. "What was going on?" they would ask, but they got no reply.

Part of the problem may have centered on the fact that Tanya had lost Michael Tovar, one of her only true friends from her wild West Coast days. Their relationship had stood up through both ups and downs. She had figured that he would be there to fix her hair when it was white and they were both old. Yet one of the few people who had never abused or used her, had died. She had lost him to AIDS.

Tovar's death seemed to hit Tanya very hard. The feelings and sense of mortality overwhelmed her for a while. When she finally faced what was troubling her, she told *Country Spirit*, "It jolted me. It made me realize that I wasn't as strong as I thought I was, and that I wasn't being strong enough in other areas. There were a lot of things going on in my life . . . emotional pressure, personal pressure. And going through death is very hard for me. I haven't lost a lot of people I love, and it was really, really tough. I was looking at like, everyday that goes by, I'm a little closer to losing something I love. Every day that my dog gets older, he gets closer to dying . . . The death of a friend makes you realize you're not going to live forever, either. I did a lot of spiritual searching and with the help of the Lord and a few good friends, I finally got turned back around."

In the wake of Tovar's death Tanya quickly moved to the front of the AIDS movement. This was something that almost all other Nashville performers had shied away from in the past. She cut a PSA (public service announcement) for the AIDS Action Committee. Joining her with the plea was Mario Van Peebles, Marky Mark, Rosanna Arquette, and Richard Simmons. MTV and the Playboy Channel aired the cuts.

This controversial and courageous stand allowed Tanya to once again move forward while feeling as if she were doing something special for an old friend. Still, she wasn't blessed with a quick return to sunshine and flowers. She fell in her bus shower on the way to an Idaho show and injured her tail bone. She was in pain but kept going.

Sharon Sontag of the *Southam Star Network* (Canada), followed Tanya through a long day during this period and built on what had become so obvious to friends and family. "[Tanya] had been running herself ragged since she set her sights on stardom at age nine." Sontag then added. "With lines etched deep around her eyes and her sentences punctuated with long sighs, it's obvious that this hardworking single mom is in dire need of a break. 'It isn't easy to have a career and have a family, it's a constant effort to have it all,' she says, adding that her situation is not unique."

But in all honesty it was unique. She was a working mom who hit dates six hundred miles apart day after day, night after night. At a time when she was making enough money to buy a nice new upper-middle class home each and every week, she rarely saw the farm she so loved. Her kids were spending more and more time with folks and less and less time with her. And her folks were often at their new place in West Virginia. It seemed that the more she had to share, the more success she had earned, the less time she had to spend with the people she really loved. It was as if success were drowning her.

"You know the old saying," she told friends who begged her to take it easy, " 'If you don't do it yourself, it don't get done.' I do pretty much everything, from keep the band together, to getting to the shows, to performing, to doing interviews. It's a ninety hour a day job." The last thing Tanya needed was something to complicate that job, but as was always the case, when the tabloids ran out of story ideas, they called on Tanya. What they dug up this time was a reach.

At the supermarket checkout stands the papers cried out about Tanya's affair with Billy Ray Cyrus. That was just what she needed. Cyrus was controversial and probably a flash in the pan. The Nashville establishment didn't care for him. Tanya had no business nor any interest in getting involved with someone like Cyrus, yet because of the two of them appearing in Dolly Parton's *Romeo* video, they were linked. Trying to give herself some peace, Tanya announced that she indeed liked Cyrus. He was a really nice young man. But they were just friends, nothing more.

What didn't help her claim was when police were called to her home because of a robbery report and found Billy Ray Cyrus outside. He had broken one of Tanya's windows with a shoe. It took a lot of explaining for Tanya to clear him with the suspicious authorities. "He took me home," she told the police, "and had to help me break into my house because I forgot my key." It seemed the two had worked together that evening and Cyrus had indeed offered to take her home. That was all there was to it. Still, the gossip wheels began to turn and they didn't come to a halt until it became apparent that Tanya and Cyrus were not going to make another appearance together. At this point they were both much too busy.

Tanya had now hit the point where she was so hot that everyone wanted to spend time with her. No longer was it just her family and the crazies she had to worry about, her dressing room was usually filled with famous guests. There were sports stars, actors, members of the network, news media, writers, producers, filmmakers and other musicians. They all wanted to go out to eat, talk all night about trendy things, and many of the younger men wanted to add Tanya to their list of conquests. She was now beginning to know what it was like to wish to be a "Female Elvis" and have that wish granted. She must have wondered where all these people were when she was lonely, hungry and had wanted to party. Right now she just wanted them to move on out and give her time with her children.

Time, something she had sung about for years, was her most elusive commodity. When measured against fame and fortune, she now knew that time was far more valuable. Yet there was so much to do, so many places she had to be, so many people who wanted a piece of her. She had fought hard to get to the top of the mountain, to be accepted for who she was and what she had accomplished. Now surrounded by all kinds of people who just wanted to bask in her glow for a few minutes, she had to wonder if it had all been worth it.

Of course the answer was yes. This is what she had dreamed of for over twenty years. It had been her goal. This had been the plateau she had dreamed of reaching, the status which had eluded her for so long, and it was worth it. But she needed to get it under a tighter control before she lost the one thing she wanted to give her children, the best years of her life.

Chapter Eighteen

Very Soon

She's one of the best draws we have. She's the
epitome of a dynamic and energetic entertainer.
—*Robert Gallagher, Director of Entertainment*
  Billy Bob's, The World's Biggest Honky Tonk

*T*anya had begun the previous year by landing on *People*'s best-dressed list. She started this one making the much better known Mr. Blackwell's list. Joining her were Julia Roberts, Glenn Close, La Toya Jackson, Susan Sarandon, Rosie Perez, Holly Hunter, Rosie O'Donnell and Daryl Hannah. In announcing his "34th Annual Worst-Dressed List" the critic described Tanya as "a tornado—trapped in a truck stop." While many would have questioned just how she could go from best to worst in just a few months when she was still wearing the same type of clothes, no one questioned why Tanya's style reminded Blackwell of a tornado. After all Tanya had been identified with a major storm for a generation now. She was one of the most powerful and unpredictable forces in country music, and it appeared that she was going to continue to be so for some time.

Tanya took the worst-dressed award with about as much good-natured enthusiasm as she had the best-dressed one. These bits of recognition were fun, gained solid press, but mattered little to the music career of the entertainer. The lists and the awards were nice, but she had other things she wanted more. One of them was long-term financial security.

In order to keep moving forward the star now realized that she had to reach out to new people. Fresh blood in the organization meant that she also received new ideas. During her work with Black Velvet, one public relations representative, Dixie Pineda, had impressed her a great deal. Ms. Pineda seemed to have a feel for making good press out of bad news. She even helped to figure ways to make a whiskey company look like a wholesome, responsible sponsor for her tour. This was the type of person Tanya really needed—someone who knew how to use the press to her advantage. Soon Tanya and Dixie had a solid working relationship and this led to Dixie leaving her job with a Dallas-based advertising firm and moving to Nashville to form Trifecta Entertainment. From this humble beginning Pineda quickly put together an organization which not only became the public relations machine behind Ms. Tucker, but behind a host of other up-and-coming stars as well.

Tanya's ability to spot talent and use it was one of the ways she now gave those around her breaks. It also pointed out that the star was still looking outward and ahead, not inward like so many of the other veteran Nashville stars did. As a matter of fact, Tanya didn't seem to like to look back at all. Other stars could have museums built to celebrate every moment of their careers, she wasn't interested. Except for her hits, she often just wished that her past would simply stay in the past. She was tired of questions about things that just didn't matter anymore. Yet just because she was tired of them didn't mean that they would go away. One old ghost that simply wouldn't leave her alone was Glen Campbell. About the time it seemed that the press had asked Tanya every question that could be asked on her days with Glen, Campbell wrote a book and devoted an entire chapter to raking his former lover over the coals.

At first when she was asked about her view of what Campbell had written, Tanya didn't show much reaction at all. She treated it like old, boring news. She attempted to ignore it, hoping it would go away. Yet because of his deeply personal and scathing attacks in *Rhinestone Cowboy,* in time Tanya had to acknowledge she had been hurt. As Glen went on the talk show circuit and devoted much of his time to drilling her, Tanya was forced to finally speak out. Still, while defending herself, she didn't aim any of her attacks directly at Glen. She continued to try and take the high road.

"There are things I could be bitter about," she admitted, "but what the hell. It wouldn't do any good." She was hoping that this story would get old in a hurry and simply go away. The tabloids and Campbell made sure it didn't. They both continued to talk about it, with Tanya being made out to be the villain.

Finally Tanya had taken all she could. She began to briefly touch on Glen's book in her interviews. She admitted for the first time that she was bitter over the fact that Glen Campbell was using her to sell books. She could not believe that he had told so many secrets, but what hurt her more was that he had also slanted the story to make her look like the devil incarnate. Glen, the man who had almost cost her her career, the man who had taken her heart and broken it with lies about love, had tried in his book to make it look as if he were the abused person rather than the abuser.

What burned Tanya even more was Campbell's claim that he had now turned his life around thanks to a newfound Christian commitment. Glen's claim of a newfound saintly image didn't sit well with Tanya. She publicly stated that she didn't want Campbell's kind of Christianity. If that was how a Christian acted, then she would go another way. Yet in a very real sense, Tanya then turned around and showed a whole lot of Christian compassion to Glen. Rather than tie into Glen's book and expose the inconsistencies in his story, Tanya bit her tongue and continued her long held stance not to say negative things about others in public. Glen could live with the lies she indicated he had told, she would turn the other cheek.

Closing the book on Glen, Tanya added that if she ever wrote her story, then people would find out the truth, but all she cared about at this moment was letting them know that they were only hearing one side of the story. And that side, she claimed, had not been very accurately remembered. With that noted, she went back to her jobs of mother and entertainer. To the surprise of many, the job of mother seemed to now be the most important one to her.

It was probably this maternal drive, the desire to watch and be with her children every chance she had, that was now causing Tanya to once again feel the pressure of being a star. And it wasn't just the push from the common everyday concert goer that was getting to her, it was the backstage rush of "important star" types. These people were robbing her of time with her own children. When the show was over she wanted to be treated just like everyone else who had a job. She liked to go home and relax but she couldn't do it. Everyone wanted a moment with her.

In spite of the fact that she was beginning to resent these stolen hours, she would not walk away from a child who wanted an autograph. And while she may have disliked the constant grabbing and pulling of fans and the media, she still responded to it in a positive fashion. Unlike a few years before when she was struggling to find direction and often missing shows, she now knew and respected that it was the fans who stuck with her through thick and thin and gave her the life she now enjoyed. They had every right to reach for a piece of her. In a sense, they owned her. They put her back on top, and she was very grateful. But she had had enough of the famous hanger-oners. She had also had enough of the groupies. She wanted some time for her children, and these people had no right to steal that time from her. More and more the former party girl attempted to distance herself from these types. But time or not, she wouldn't distance herself from her fans.

In an attempt to make sure that she had the opportunity to let each fan know just how much she appreciated them, Tanya put LaCosta in charge of her fan club. With her sister overseeing the mail, the requests and the special needs, she was assured that nothing important would fall through the cracks. If Tanya needed to send a card or make a call, LaCosta would make sure she knew about it.

The fact that LaCosta was there also allowed Tanya to feel that she could sneak away more often for time with the kids. With her sister caring for the fan clubs, a bit of the pressure was off the star. It was at least one area of her life where she didn't have to wonder if all that needed to be done was getting done. She knew that it was.

By bringing on people like LaCosta and Dixie, Tanya was showing a great deal of savvy and maturity. She was becoming a businesswoman who realized that she had to delegate power. She would place that power only in the hands of good people she could trust. By building an organization of solid professionals who cared about her as much as their jobs, who would be honest with her even if it meant telling her she was wrong, she was assured that positive things would be accomplished. Her own time would no longer be wasted in areas which really didn't need a great deal of her input freeing up more time to think about her kids.

Although raised in a fishbowl and catered to by so many who wanted to be in Tanya's good graces, the star's children were anything but spoiled in the negative sense of the word. They were outgoing, polite and comfortable around people of all ages. They were bright kids who knew how to charm an audience, and like their mother, they seemed to enjoy the spotlight.

Tanya would often bring them out on stage with her at the end of her shows. She wanted the crowd to meet them. She wanted the fans to applaud and approve of her children the same way they approved of her. In a way these two little ones were Tanya's medals, and they were much more important to her than gold records or awards. This girl and boy were all hers and she held them as only a mother would do—selfishly. She wrapped them in her arms as if they were a treasure. And to her they were.

The Tanya who still loved to travel, the Tanya who still loved cities like New York and Chicago, the Tanya who followed the NFL Bears and Cowboys, loved horse shows, and tried to make time to go places like Oprah Winfrey's restaurant, The Eccentric, would now rather talk about her children than herself or her career. When she related her stories, she also probed others about how she was going to avoid the pitfalls of raising children in such a strange life-style. She wanted input, she wanted insight. She wanted to be the world's greatest mom.

Tanya often admitted that she was worried about her children growing up rich. She was concerned that having money and expensive things would make them strangers to their roots. Tanya wondered if she just shouldn't walk away from the business and move to a rural house and have a normal life-style.

There were times when she sounded sure of her need to place motherhood above career. These moments were when she found herself on the road without her children. During those lonely times she vowed that while it was going to take at least two more years of hard travel before she could cut back, when that time came she was going to spend a great deal more time with her children than she did on the road. Yet for now it was the road and Black Velvet that seemed to own her.

Diane Jennings of the *Dallas Morning News* asked Tanya during a tour if she wanted her daughter to grow up as she had. Did she want her to be on the road, working crowds and being part of the show business scene? It didn't take Tanya long to answer. "I don't think it should be encouraged, but I'm not going to discourage it either. She makes her own decisions. I just think it's not for everybody. I would much rather her be in a little more stable business."

A few days later, when asked the same question about her children, Tanya added, "I'm gonna let it be God's will for whatever they choose to do. I'm not gonna really encourage them but I certainly won't discourage it."

Deep down one had to question if Tanya would want anyone to make the sacrifices and go through the pain that she had. Especially now that Glen's book was bringing so many bad and long-buried memories and horror stories back to the top. Just like her father once had, she wanted to sacrifice to help her children find their dreams. And just like Beau had, she prayed that neither of these kids would have to suffer in the ways she had. Above everything else, she wanted to protect them from that. Tanya knew that only time would tell, and her time with them was racing by ever so quickly.

As much as she would like to run away with her children for a few months, she couldn't. Others needed her too. So it was always back to work. In the studio Tanya was toiling harder than ever. Still in an overdrive mode, she wanted her next album to be her best ever. Tanya listened to over three thousand demos to find the songs for this new project. She wanted to make sure that everything was right, that this album was something to again build on, not the first step on the downhill side of her career. With the material that she had picked which she believed was the best ever, and with Jerry at the controls and aware of her goals, she believed that she could pull off a masterpiece.

When enough time has passed to evaluate this album's real lasting effect, the critics might just mark "Soon" as having been a major turning point in the mature Tanya's career. In the midst of Glen Campbell trying to remind everyone about the old wild Tanya, this album seemed to take a more settled woman and bring out her softer side. "Soon" even had a bit of a soulful feel to it. The record was both smooth and deep. It seemed to come from a gentler heart than any of the other Tucker albums.

The CD and tapes hit stores around Tanya's thirty-fifth birthday. And while like most of Tanya's past work, it was still fun and a bit on the edge, it was also different. In a very subtle way it was more mellow. The one thing it wasn't, and Tanya fans everywhere seemed pleased, was controversial.

The first single was the album's title cut. The song spoke of a woman being alone for the holidays without the man she loved. In a very real way, even surrounded by her own family, Tanya was also alone with no real love. Her family members were happily married, and she couldn't even find a special man for her life. It seemed that now that she had industry recognition, the one thing missing was someone to love and cherish forever. She must have felt the message of this song as strongly as those who listened to it. In a way it must have haunted her.

Even if the song's message didn't haunt Tanya, the video certainly would. Tanya had once again made Ben Reed a part of the project. She had also filmed a bedroom scene that would be far hotter than anything ever seen on TNN or CMT. In one segment of the video Reed and Tucker were nude and in bed. It was ironic that the normally out-front and open Tanya had the set cleared to shoot these nude scenes. Some on the crew remarked that she wasn't nearly as brazen as she was thought to be.

Liberty didn't know how well the nudity, with most of the important body parts casually covered with sheets, would fly in the country market, so they asked Tanya to reshoot the scene a second time. This allowed them to cover a part of Tanya's breast which had been shown in the hotter release. The record label then offered the country music networks both versions of the video and let them decide which they wanted to air. It came as no surprise that TNN and CMT went for the tamer release.

Even though it wasn't being aired, the mere fact that a hot version had been filmed set tongues wagging. Tanya was again flaunting convention and the establishment was again getting nervous. The talk about the scene and the controversy it created guaranteed two things. The first was a hit record and the second was Tanya getting a great deal of press coverage. As always, Tanya used it to her full advantage.

Ironically the hot video, the one which wasn't aired, was not really "R" rated. What played out in those black-and-white images would not have been questioned if it aired on network television during the day-time soaps. "NYPD Blue" and a host of other nighttime shows were much hotter. So why all the controversy?

For starters it was because of Tanya. She was controversial and many members of the moral majority loved to single her out and attack her. A part of it was also due to TNN and CMT wanting to maintain a very clean, family oriented reputation. And finally it was due to the fact that both the star and the label realized that if they filmed a "secret" hot version and couldn't get it aired, then folks would immediately demand to know what all the fuss was about. In other words, it would assure them a hit. Did "Soon" need all of this to become a major hit album? It probably would have done just fine without any help. It was that good. But the rush from the publicity sure did allow it to take off in a hurry.

"Soon" spurred on by the talk and press created by

the controversial video, climbed the charts through the end of 1993 and topped out at a place the star was now used to. With this record, Tanya now had hit #2 with five of her last seven recordings. It was also the ninth time in her career she had been stopped one slot from the top. Still, with so much ink and video coverage, the public would have sworn that it was a #1.

The critics and fans loved the record. Susan Beyer, writing for the *Ottawa Citizen* probably summed up the overall view of the press. "Right now Tanya Tucker is the best, bar none, and she's got her place in country music pantheon firmly secured for all time."

A few weeks later Tanya was named CMT's 1993 Video Artist of the Year. Steady at the top, firmly in control of her organization and material, Tanya was as hot as she had ever been, but was that still important to her? Would the call of motherhood divert her attention enough to push her off the road and out of the spotlight? Did she still want to make the sacrifice that a life in the spotlight demanded?

- Chapter Nineteen -

Looking Down the Road

Being anywhere near a wedding gown makes me nervous.

—Tanya Tucker

Going into 1994 Tanya Tucker was ranked thirty-sixth on Billboard's list of all-time top country music artists. She was graded ahead of female stars and legends such as Reba McEntire, Crystal Gayle, Barbara Mandrell and Dottie West. The only women to rank above Tanya were Dolly Parton, #8; Loretta Lynn, #17; Tammy Wynette, #23; and Kitty Wells at #31. Of these only Dolly was now having any consistent chart success. With Tanya still going strong, she should continue to move up the ladder in the rankings of country music's female legends. Even if she never records another single or album, she will climb past Wells into third place. If she remains active for just five more years, who knows how high she will eventually go?

A decade ago no one would have predicted that Tanya Tucker would now rate as one of the top recording artists of all time. Back then a more likely view was that her abusive habits would have kept her from ever recording again. Yet in the face of severe odds, Tanya came back time and time again and become a real superstar. By the beginning of 1994 she was such a top-flight act that she not only caught the eyes of those who listened to and observed country music, but the whole world too!

Tanya was chosen to head a lineup of country music all-stars at Super Bowl XXVIII. Her old beau Jim Kelly might have been tossing footballs for the Bills, and a hot new country act, Travis Tritt, might be joining her on stage, but it was Tanya who had the most famous name. She was the real superstar at the superbowl.

Following acts like Whitney Houston and Michael Jackson, as well as Garth Brooks and the Judds, must have given Tanya a real sense of justice. She once had tried to bolt from country music in order to reach a wider audience. She had then been shunned because she had wanted to be accepted by more people and become an entertainer who was looked upon as special in a number of different areas. She wanted to be ranked up there with Elvis. There was still no one who ranked with the King, but Tanya had reached that long wished for goal of being accepted and recognized by the masses. Ironically she managed to come up to Jackson/Houston acceptance standards by first going home to Nashville and country music. Yet her superbowl spotlight was almost extinguished before it was turned on by the wild stories of her youth now remembered and brought into sharp focus in Glen Campbell's autobiography.

"At first the NFL said I was too wild," Tanya recalled. Being considered too wild for a football crowd was something Tanya had problems believing. The league was filled with men who had abused drugs and alcohol, scores of them had been tossed in jail for fighting and others had bulked up their bodies on substances that were probably far worse than anything the singer had tried in even her darkest days. She was insulted that the NFL media consultants would look at her as being a worse influence than their own players. So she informed Beau, "Tell them that I don't need football. I've been here twenty years and I don't need it. If they think I'm too wild then get somebody else!"

A few days later the NFL came back and informed her they had reconsidered. They wanted her. They begged her to forgive them. After making them stew for a while, she did.

A few weeks later Tanya lighted up the field and made the halftime show a lot more interesting than the Cowboy's victory over the Bills. But when the game was over it was probably Buffalo with whom Tanya could most identify. After all she had been considered a loser far more than a winner for most of her career. The winning days had come only after a lot of trips down disappointment alley. If the Bills were like this country singer, they would simply regroup and do it all again until they got it right. When that happened, the old days would be a little easier to accept.

With Campbell's book losing popularity and with his new Branson theater not pulling in the huge crowds he had expected, Tanya had few problems accepting and living with the present and the *Rhinestone Cowboy*'s talk of the old days. After all, past glory might be all that Glen had to hang his hat on. To her it must have seemed that justice was finally being served. After all, she was hot and those who threw stones were not.

Besides a tour schedule that would take her all over the United States in 270 days, an album that was going to go gold and platinum, and two growing children, Tanya had so many other things to keep her busy that it seemed the world was always knocking at her door with flowers and candy. While she still resented giving up so much of her time, she did love to be wanted.

Sporting a trim, hard and sexy body, she decided she needed to exploit the fact that she had two children, a busy life and was still in top shape. Going into the studio she worked with Sindy Benson, a personal trainer, and together they brought to life an idea which had been festering in Tanya's mind for more than a decade. With fitness model Lisa Rice leading the action and the *Firm*

Buns folks, the Maier Group producing and distributing the product, Tanya released the *Tanya Tucker Country Workout*. This low-impact aerobics video immediately became one of the top-selling fitness videos on the market. For those who loved Tanya's music (her hits served as the background for all the routines) the fifty-minute session was a great way to get in shape.

On the talk shows Tanya explained just how the idea came to her. "My career as a country singer has kept me on the road for the better part of twenty years. Over the years, I've come up with a workout program that helps me firm up all over and gives me the energy I need to keep up my hectic pace. My workout routine has made me feel so great that I want to share it with others."

Surprising some in country music, the workout gathered good reviews from fitness magazines. This gave Tanya a spotlight to shine on another of her new pet ventures.

Even back when she was trying to make a go of it with Glen Campbell, Tanya had dreamed of developing her own line of clothing. Glen started and then stopped financing her first attempt. The next time she tried it, the jeans she designed simply didn't obtain enough exposure at the marketplace. Now the timing seemed right.

PFI, the country's largest western wear store and one of the nation's biggest western catalog distributors, contacted the country singer. They wanted Tanya to design a moderately priced line of clothes that would reflect her own taste for both dress and casual wear. They guaranteed her that they would advertise and promote the product if she would endorse and stand behind it. When they put their offer in writing, Tanya didn't have to be asked twice to sign on the dotted line.

The Tanya Tucker Collection initially ranged from casual wear, including denim jeans and western shirts, to striking skirts and blazers, and was it successful. PFI did more than $5 million in sales on the line of clothes in

1994. Randy Little, owner and president of PFI was so impressed with the star's feel for the market that he couldn't say enough nice things about her. "Tanya had a good idea of what she was going for when we met," he explained when asked who he had wanted to sign on so quickly. "She wanted great-looking clothes that were comfortable and fun, not stuffy old items . . . but she wanted them all at reasonable prices."

The clothes were top-notch in style, but more importantly, the prices ranged from as little as fifteen to just over ninety dollars. Due to their initial success, the Home Shopping Club asked to get involved. Tanya and HSC thus began to carve out open dates in her schedule so that she could join Vanna White, Connie Stephens and Louise Mandrell in Florida once a month to hawk products and make money.

Jumping back onto the video screen, Tanya churned out a flashing, fun offering for her latest single, "Hangin' In." The upbeat video, with its modern beach setting, was soon climbing the charts as rapidly as her first release from the "Soon" album. And in this video everybody had their clothes on. There were no "R" rated versions. "Hangin' In" hung on the Billboard all the way to the top five in August.

Somehow Tanya also found the time to jump into other recording studios and duet with such superstars as Frank Sinatra, Kenny Rogers and Little Richard. Appearing with Sinatra was a huge thrill and great for her ego, but working with Little Richard was a whole lot more fun. Tanya was also asked to join in on the "Common Threads" tribute/benefit for Walden Woods. Almost everyone who was anyone in Nashville was a part of this platinum album that featured the music of the country/rock band, the Eagles.

In spite of the heavy work load, Tanya somehow looked more relaxed and younger than she had in years. Rumors running around Nashville were that she had undergone a face-lift. Maybe she had, but fans argued that the happiness she currently felt coupled with a new healthier life-style was now finally being seen on her face and in her eyes. That is what had happened to her crow's-feet. For one of the first times in her life, Tanya wasn't talking. And if Dolly wouldn't explain her "beauty" secrets, why should Tanya have to.

No matter how much work she had on her plate, no matter how much time it took to set up for huge shows at venues as large as Texas Stadium, no matter how much she needed her "beauty" sleep to keep her new younger look intact, Tanya was not going to be denied the opportunity to get some time astride a horse. With only a few hours to practice and riding a borrowed mount, she won the National Cutting Horse Association's annual Futurity in Fort Worth, Texas. Then, just a few weeks later, one of her Arabians, Tanya Tucker's Dream, won Grand Reserve Champion at a Scottsdale, Arizona, horse show. As always, Tanya was a cowboy's dream, only who was the cowboy?

As Tanya readied to entertain the world at the opening ceremonies of the World Cup, she stated that she wanted to have at least one more child. She really enjoyed being a mother, and she would love to hold one more child to her breast. This time she seemed to want to obtain that goal in a less radical fashion. She didn't seem to want to bring her children's designated father, Ben Reed, back into the picture. Now, more than ever, she wanted someone to love and share all of the wonderful things in her life. To understand just what love meant to a life, she only had to look at her parents.

The star who couldn't find the right man, felt she needed to honor her folks in a special way that would allow her to publicly tell them how proud she was that they had stuck together for all these years. While performing on the huge cruise ship the SS *Norway*, Tanya secretly set up a fifty-year wedding celebration for her parents. She flew in scores of their friends and relatives, and then surprised them at a dinner by having the captain remarry them. Tanya underwrote the entire cost just so she could put her parents and their successful union in the spotlight. With the media in attendance, she bragged constantly about how wonderful it was to have loved someone that long and stayed with them through thick and thin.

Then she added, "May I present Mr. and Mrs. Beau Tucker again."

The look in Tanya's eyes said it all. As the family posed for pictures, those around her sensed that all the pain and effort of twenty plus years on the road and in the studio was worth it because it provided the means to make this day special. And even though she kept saying that she got too nervous to be around a wedding too often, it also seemed obvious that she would like to find that kind of love for her life. Especially now that she had so much to share. At every new corner there seemed to be another honor or another chance for a very special time.

Tanya was the first country star on the Dallas Hard Rock Cafe's "Walk of Fame." Then, in an act that was probably twenty years too late, the Country Music Walk of Fame in Nashville welcomed her to the CMA Hall of Fame building. In accepting the honor she centered her praise on her father. She also mentioned those who had produced her records, but mainly she wanted the fans to know how much she owed them for sticking by her—for keeping her career afloat. She also thanked the Good Lord.

In 1994 Tanya seemed more bent on a spiritual comfort than a quest for awards or gold records. She felt a need to expand a part of her that might have been neglected for too long. She didn't want to end up like old Hank Williams. The music legend whose great compositions included "I Saw the Light," told Minnie Pearl just weeks before he died, "That's the problem, Minnie. There just ain't no light." Tanya knew there had to be a light even brighter than the stage's spotlight, and she wanted to experience it too.

She told *Country Fever's* Neil Haislop in 1994, "I went to church and vacation Bible school [as a child]. I definitely am a spiritual person. I believe Jesus was the son of God, I believe all that, and I believe in the Bible. Unfortunately, what we end up developing last is our spirituality, because after we get all that other stuff, it's like, 'Okay, there's something missing.' So, I think probably that's something I'm going to be working on in my future, not just for me, but for my children. The best thing is being a good example."

So once again it came back to her motherhood. The woman who defied description for so long was now looking to find a way to be a role model for her own children. Maybe for the very first time she really did care what people thought and where her life was ultimately headed.

She told *Total Health*, "I definitely think the good Lord leads and helps me in the direction I should go. I am very spiritually minded. Someday I would love to do a gospel album." This search for direction had led Tanya to deepen her friendship with Paul Overstreet. Rarely did a week go by when the two didn't find time to talk about the Lord and His place for Tanya.

Is she ever going to settle down, get married and become Nashville's version of normal? Not even Tanya knows the answer, but she is looking. And over the course of the last decade, in spite of a life-style that frequently shocked people, she had been honest enough and straightforward enough to gain Music City's respect. That in itself was a huge step for a young woman who once couldn't get the time of day from Nashville's writers or music executives.

Neil Haislop wrote of Tanya in *The World of Country*

Music, "She's the kind of person you want on your side and in your life. Fiercely loyal, she is generous to a fault, and would never refuse a favor." And that was the way she had been even in her most troubled times. So maybe she has always been more spiritual, closer to her Lord, than anyone, including Tanya herself could admit.

So, once again, who is Tanya Tucker?

The veteran star whose career seems destined to outlive some of the country's newest stars told David Zimmerman of the Gannet News Service, "Some people think I'm wild and crazy, some think I'm very much a homebody, and some think I'm a rock 'n' roller. I guess I can be all of those things."

My personal guess is that Tanya Tucker will be around for many more years, shocking us, thrilling us and pushing the limits a bit further than anyone in Nashville ever dared to before country music saw the arrival of "The Texas Tornado."

THE STORIES BEHIND THE MUSIC

YOUR CHEATIN' HEART: A BIOGRAPHY OF HANK WILLIAMS
Chet Flippo
_____ 95103-5 $4.99 U.S./$5.99 Can.
He sang racy honky-tonk songs next to tender gospel ballads. This rags-to-riches story of the first "Cadillac Cowboy" includes never-before-published material on Williams' daughter.

COUNTRY MUSIC BABYLON
Jeff Rovin
_____ 95027-6 $4.99 U.S./$5.99 Can.
An explosive exposé that tells you what the tabloids won't about Billy Ray Cyrus, Kenny Rogers, Garth Brooks, Hank Williams and many more.

HONKY TONK ANGEL: THE INTIMATE STORY OF PATSY CLINE
Ellis Nassour
_____ 95158-2 $5.99 U.S./$6.99 Can.
She walked the line between sinner and saint; but when she sang, she was an angel. Read all about her career, her image, her money, her men, her music.

THERE'S NEVER BEEN A TRAVEL GUIDE QUITE LIKE THIS ONE!

BRANSON and BEYOND
Kathryn Buckstaff

A COUNTRY MUSIC LOVER'S GUIDE TO VISITING:

- BRANSON, MISSOURI: Home to over 30 music shows and theaters—the new center of live country music performance!
- NASHVILLE: "Music City U.S.A." and home of the Grand Ole Opry!
- PIGEON FORGE, TENNESSEE: Where country and bluegrass come together with Dollywood and the Smoky Mountains!

Where to stay, what to see, places to shop, where to eat, and, of course, where to go for America's finest country music experiences!

BRANSON AND BEYOND
Kathryn Buckstaff
_____ 95092-6 $4.99 U.S./$5.99 Can.

Naomi Judd and her daughter Wynonna shocked the world when they announced they'd be ending their seven-year career together. Despite her spirited performances at dozens of sold-out concerts, Naomi's battle with a life-threatening disease was forcing her into retirement—leaving Wynonna to carry on the family tradition. But this was not the first time Naomi had fought the odds and won....

Here is an honest, in-depth look at the lives of Naomi and Wynonna Judd—the early years of struggle, the super-star years as the queens of country music, and their heart-rending personal tragedies. For their millions of devoted fans, THE JUDDS is a rare glimpse into the lives of two remarkable women.

The Unauthorized Biography

BOB MILLARD